Professional Paper P2
Corporate Reporting (International and UK)

First edition 2007, Tenth edition April 2015

ISBN 9781 4727 2706 0

e ISBN 9781 4727 2771 8

British Library Cataloguing-in-Publication Data
A catalogue record for this book is available from the British Library

Published by

BPP Learning Media Ltd,
BPP House, Aldine Place,
142-144 Uxbridge Road,
London W12 8AA

Printed in the UK by
Ashford Colour Press Ltd

Unit 600
Fareham Reach
Gosport
Hampshire PO13 0FW

www.bpp.com/learningmedia

Your learning materials, published by BPP Learning Media Ltd, are printed on paper obtained from traceable sustainable sources.

Welcome to BPP Learning Media's new syllabus ACCA **Passcards for Professional Paper P2 Corporate Reporting (International and UK Stream)**.

- They **focus on your exam** and **save you time**.
- They incorporate **diagrams** to kick start your memory.
- They follow the overall **structure** of BPP Learning Media's Study Texts, but BPP Learning Media's ACCA **Passcards** are not just a condensed book. Each card has been separately designed for clear presentation. Topics are self contained and can be grasped visually.
- ACCA **Passcards** are still **just the right size** for pockets, briefcases and bags.

Run through the **Passcards** as often as you can during your final revision period. The day before the exam, try to go through the **Passcards** again! You will then be well on your way to passing your exams.

Good luck!

		Page
1	Financial reporting framework	1
2	Professional and ethical duty of the accountant	7
3	Non-current assets	13
4	Employee benefits	25
5	Provisions, contingencies and EARP	33
6	Income taxes	37
7	Financial instruments	43
8	Leases	59
9	Share-based payment	65
10	Performance reporting	69
11	Related parties	87
12	Revision of basic groups	91
13	Complex groups and joint arragements	105
14	Changes in group structures	113
15	Continuing and discontinued interests	119
16	Foreign currency transactions and entities	123
17	Group statements of cash flows	131
18	Environmental and social reporting	137
19	Current developments	149
20	Reporting for specialised entities	155
21	Reporting for small and medium-sized entities	163

1: Financial reporting framework

Topic List

- Regulatory framework
- Conceptual framework
- Revenue recognition

This chapter sets the scene for your Corporate Reporting studies.

The reporting environment changes constantly through new regulations, standards etc

International influences are increasing, through the IASB and multinational business.

Regulatory framework

International Accounting Standards

IASC Foundation
↓
Trustees
↓
- International Accounting Standards Board (IASB)
- Standing Interpretations Committee (SIC)
- Standards Advisory Council (SAC)

European Union

Listed companies have complied with IAS since 2005.

Stock Exchange

National Listing Rules to be complied with by listed companies.

Other

National laws

- Take precedence over IFRS/IAS

OECD

- Undertakes its own research into accounting standards, via ad hoc working groups, issuing guidelines for members

Conceptual framework – a statement of generally accepted theoretical principles which form the frame of reference for financial reporting.

Advantages	Disadvantages
☑ Avoids 'patchwork' or firefighting approach	☒ Financial statements are intended for a variety of users – single framework may not suit all
☑ Less open to criticism of political/external pressure	☒ May need different standards for different purposes
☑ Some standards may concentrate on the income statement, others on the SOFP	☒ Preparing and implementing standards is still difficult with a framework

IASB Conceptual Framework

The IASB *Framework for the Preparation and Presentation of Financial Statements* was produced in 1989 and is gradually being replaced by the new *Conceptual Framework for Financial Reporting.*

It is a joint IASB/FASB project and is being produced in phases.

- *Phase 1:* Chapters 1 and 3, published in September 2010
  - Chapter 1: *The objective of general purpose financial reporting*
  - Chapter 3: *Qualitative characteristics of useful financial information*
- Chapter 2 *The Reporting Entity* has not yet been published and is still an ED
- Chapter 4 includes the remaining chapters of the 1989 *Framework:*
  - Underlying assumption
  - The elements of financial statements
  - Recognition of the elements of financial statements
  - Measurement of the elements of financial statements
  - Concepts of capital and capital maintenance
- Discussion paper issued in July 2013 proposing topical areas for revision and amendment

IFRS 15

Revenue is that which arises in the course of ordinary activities such as that from sales, services provided, interest, royalties and dividends.

Includes only those amounts receivable by the entity on its own account. Not sales, goods and sales tax collected by agent to be passed to the principal.

Measurement

- **Fair value** of consideration received/receivable. Deferred amounts discounted
- In a sale financed by the seller, any difference between the fair value of the item and the nominal sales value should be accounted for as interest revenue

Recent developments

IFRS 15 *Revenue from contracts with customers* was issued in 2014. The core principle is that an entity should 'recognise revenue to depict the the transfer of promised goods or services in an amount that reflects the consideration to which the entity expects to be entitled'.

Recognition

Goods

IFRS15 details a five step process for revenue recognition:

1. Identify the contract with a customer
2. Identify the performance obligations in the contract
3. Determine the transaction price
4. Alllocate the transaction price to performance obligations
5. Recognise revenue when performance obligations are satisfied

Services

- Conditions 1 to 5 as for goods
- Certain performance obligations are satisfied over time (mainly services) rather than at a point in time. Measure performance to date using output and input methods
- Interest – time proportion basis (effective yield)
- Royalties – accruals basis
- Dividends – when the right to the dividend is established

Disclosure

Accounting policy for each recognition; the amount of each significant category of revenue; amount of revenue from exchange of goods or services.

2: Professional and ethical duty of the accountant

Topic List

- Ethical theories
- Individual influences
- Ethics in organisations
- Professional ethics
- Ethics in the exam

Ethics are an important part of the ACCA qualification. This chapter is concerned with the professional integrity of the accountant and director.

Lack of objective standards

Non-cognitivism – no possibility of acquiring objective knowledge of moral principles.

Moral relativism – right and wrong are culturally determined.

Teleological Consequentalist ethics

Moral judgements based on outcomes or consequences. Utilitarianism means acting for the greatest good to the greatest number.

Egoism

Act is ethically justified if decision-makers pursue short-term desires or long-term interests (justification for free market).

Objective standards

Cognitivism – objective, universal principles exist and can be known, ethics can be regarded as absolute.

Deontological ethics

Kant stated that acts can be judged in advance by moral criteria:

- Do what others should be doing
- Treat people as autonomous beings and not as means to an end
- Act as if acting in accordance with universal laws

Pluralism

Different views may exist but it should be possible to reach a consensus; morality is a social phenomenon.

National and cultural beliefs

Differences lie in four main areas.

- Role of individual v collective good
- Acceptance of power distribution
- Desire to avoid uncertainty
- Masculinity v femininity (money/possessions v people/relationships)

Education and employment

People's education/work background seems to be more significant with globalisation.

Morality

Actions are influenced not only by people's own integrity but also how much awareness they have of their actions' moral consequences.

Psychological factors

Focus is on how people think and how they decide what is morally right and wrong.

Locus of control

Influence individuals believe they have over their own lives.

- **Internal** – individuals have significant influence
- **External** – lives shaped by luck/circumstances

Moral development

Kohlberg's three levels – ethics determined by:

1. Rewards/punishments (Pre-conventional)
2. Others' expectations (Conventional)
3. Individual's own decisions (Post-conventional)

Ethics

A code of moral principles that people follow with respect to what is right or wrong

Not necessarily enforced by law

Ethical systems

- **Personal ethics** – eg deriving from upbringing or political or religious beliefs
- **Professional ethics** – eg medical ethics
- **Organisation culture**
- **Organisation systems** – may be in a formal code reinforced by the overall statement of values

Two approaches

- **Compliance based** – ensures that the company acts within the letter of the law. Violations are prevented, detected and punished
- **Integrity based** – combines a concern for the law with an emphasis on managerial responsibility for ethical behaviours. Strives to define companies' guiding values, aspirations and pattern of thought and conduct

Code of ethics and conduct

This lays out ACCA's rules stating the ethics and behaviour required by all members and **students** of the ACCA. Guidance is in the form of **fundamental principles** (see below), specific guidance statements and explanatory notes.

Integrity	Members should be straightforward and honest in all business and professional relationships.
Objectivity	Members should not allow bias, conflicts of interest or undue influence of others to override professional or business judgements.
Professional competence and due care	Members have a continuing duty to maintain professional knowledge and skill at a level required to ensure that a client or employer receives competent professional service based on current developments in practice, legislation and techniques. Members should act diligently and in accordance with applicable technical and professional standards when providing professional services.
Confidentiality	Members should respect the confidentiality of information acquired as a result of professional and business relationships and should not disclose any such information to third parties without proper or specific authority or unless there is a legal or professional right or duty to disclose. Confidential information acquired as a result of professional and business relationships should not be used for the personal advantage of members or third parties.
Professional behaviour	Members should comply with relevant laws and regulations and should avoid any action that discredits the profession.

Ethics are most likely to be considered in the context of the accountant's role as adviser to the directors.

Question 1, the case study, nearly always involves an ethical dilemma relating to 'creative' accounting.

3: Non-current assets

Topic List

- Definition of an asset
- IASs 16, 20 and 23
- Impairment
- Investment property
- IAS 38
- Goodwill

You should have met IAS 16 in your earlier studies. It is a fairly uncontroversial standard, though detailed.

IASs 20 and 23 are covered only very briefly, as they should be familiar to you.

IAS 40 Investment property *is fairly straightforward.*

The treatment of goodwill changed following the revision of IFRS 3 Business combinations.

IASB Framework: an asset is a resource controlled by an entity as a result of past events and from which future economic benefits are expected to flow to the entity

FASB (USA): assets are probable future economic benefits obtained or controlled by a particular entity as a result of past transactions or events

ASB (UK): assets are rights or other access to future economic benefits controlled by an entity as a result of past transactions or events

Key points

- Future economic benefit
- Control
- Transaction to acquire control has taken place

IAS 16 *Property, plant and equipment*

Initial measurement

On initial recognition, property, plant and equipment (PPE) is measured at its cost.

Directly attributable costs are included, eg acquisition, site preparation, installation, delivery and professional fees.

Costs of dismantling and removing the asset and restoring the site are included to the extent that they are recognised as a provision under IAS 37.

- Finance costs **must** be capitalised if they are directly attributable to the acquisition, construction or production of a qualifying asset as part of its cost
- All other borrowing costs must be expensed

PPE must be written down where necessary to its recoverable amount following IAS 36.

Subsequent expenditure (repairs and maintenance) must be **recognised in profit or loss** as it is incurred, unless:

- It enhances the economic benefits
- A component of an asset that is treated separately for depreciation purposes has been restored or replaced
- It relates to a major inspection/overhaul restoring economic benefits consumed and reflected in depreciation

Depreciation

Main points

- Depreciable amount (cost – residual value) of PPE should be allocated on a systematic basis over useful life
- Depreciation should be recognised as an expense unless included in carrying value of another asset (eg capitalising depreciation on assets used for development)

Other points

- Useful life and depreciation method should be reviewed period at least annually and adjusted for current and future periods where necessary
- Investment properties are still exempt from depreciation

Subsequent measurement

Cost model: is cost less accumulated depreciation and impairment losses. *Revaluation model:* carry at a revalued amount less subsequent accumulated depreciation/impairment losses.

Revaluation

There was a problem in the past with 'cherry picking' for revaluation. Also, valuations became out of date. Under the allowed alternative of IAS 16, revaluing assets is still optional, but:

Where a policy of revaluation is adopted, it must be applied to a whole class of assets.

The valuations must be kept up to date: annually for significant movements/volatile items, 3-5 years for other items.

Revaluations gains are credited to a revaluation surplus except to the extent that they reverse revaluation decreases of the same assets in which case – P/L for the year.

Revaluation decreases are charged

- First against any revaluation surplus relating to the same asset
- Thereafter in profit or loss

IAS 20 *Government grants*

Problems: Conflict of accruals vs prudence.
Matching is difficult.

Accounting treatment

- Matched in P/L with related costs on a systematic basis
- Grants not recognised until reasonably certain conditions of receipt complied with
- Capital grants are presented **either** as deferred income **or** by deducting grant in arriving at carrying value of asset
- Revenue grants are shown as other income or deducted from the related expense
- If repayable, accounted for as a change in accounting estimate (IAS 8), ie in current period

Accounting entries

Revenue grants
Debit Cash
Credit P/L

In expenditure period

Capital grants
Debit Cash
Credit Deferred income
Or Asset account

Release to P/L over expected useful life

IAS 23 Borrowing costs

Must be capitalised if they are directly attributable

- Other borrowing costs must be expensed

IAS 36

Only review assets for impairment if there are indicators of it, eg:

- Decline in market value
- Adverse change in market, technology, economics or law
- Increased interest rates
- Fall in value below carrying value
- Obsolescence or physical damage
- Change in use
- Poor performance

If possible test individual assets, otherwise **cash generating unit** (CGU)

Compare **carrying value** with **recoverable amount**

- An impairment loss for a CGU should be allocated
  - First to any goodwill of the CGU
  - Then to other assets on a pro-rata basis, but not below recoverable amount
- Under IAS 36, impairment losses are now recognised for intangible assets with an indefinite useful life and goodwill acquired in a business combination
- Allocation of loss with unallocated corporate assets or goodwill

  Where not all assets or goodwill have been allocated to an individual CGU then different levels of impairment tests are performed to ensure the unallocated assets are tested

Impairment losses are recognised:

- For non-revalued assets are recognised in P/L
- For revalued assets according to the relevant IFRS
- May be reversed if events causing it reverse
- An impairment loss recognised for goodwill is not reversed

Test of individual CGUs

- Then test the individual CGUs (including allocated goodwill and any portion of the carrying amount of corporate assets that can be allocated on a reasonable and consistent basis) basis

Test of group of CGUs

- Test the smallest group of CGUs that includes the CGU under review and to which the goodwill can be allocated/a portion of the carrying amount of corporate assets can be allocated on a reasonable and consistent basis

Questions are likely to involve both calculation and discussion. Impairment has come up nearly every sitting of the current syllabus.

IAS 40

An **investment property** is property (land or building) held to earn rentals or for capital appreciation or both, rather than for:

- Use in the production or supply of goods or services or for administrative purposes
- Sale in the ordinary course of business

Accounting treatment

- Choice of **fair value model** or **cost model**
- *Fair value model*
  - Revalue to fair value at each accounting date
  - Do not depreciate
  - Gain or loss to P/L
- *Cost model*
  - Follow cost model of IAS 16

Note. Leasehold investment properties are accounted for as finance leases.

Exceptions

Owner-occupied property or property held for sale to or being constructed for third parties are not investment property (IAS 16, IAS 2, IAS 11 respectively).

Disclosures

- Criteria for classification
- Assumptions in determining fair value
- Use of independent professional valuer
- Rental income and expenses
- Any restrictions or obligations

IAS 38

Intangible assets deals with research and development costs, as well as intangible assets.

Intangible asset: an identifiable non-monetary asset without physical substance held for use in the production or supply of goods or services, for rental or others, or for administrative purposes.

Development: the application of research findings or other knowledge to a plan or design for the production of new/substantially improved materials, devices, products, processes, etc.

Research: original or planned investigation undertaken with the prospect of obtaining new scientific or technical knowledge and understanding.

Internally generated brands, mastheads, publishing titles, customer lists and similar items should not be recognised as intangible assets.

Internally generated goodwill should not be recognised as an asset.

For R & D, the problem is one of matching concept vs prudence concept.

Research: original and planned investigation undertaken with the prospect of gaining new scientific or technical knowledge and understanding.

Write off as incurred

Development: use of scientific/technical knowledge in order to produce new/substantially improved materials devices, processes etc.

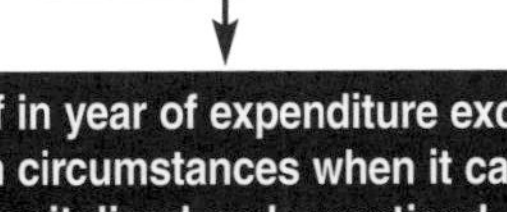

Write off in year of expenditure except in certain circumstances when it can be capitalised and amortised

Measurement

Initial measurement

- R&D, as above
- Purchased intangible assets capitalised at cost

Subsequent measurement

- *Cost model:* cost less accumulated depreciation and impairment losses
- *Revaluation model:* revaluation

Amortisation

- Systematic over useful life
- At least annual review of UL and amortisation period
- Intangibles with indefinite useful life are not amortised but reviewed at least annually for impairment

Circumstances

- **P**robable future economic benefits
- **I**ntention to complete and use/sell
- **R**esources adequate to complete and use/sell
- **A**bility to use/sell
- **T**echnical feasibility
- **E**xpenditure can be reliably measured

Goodwill can be purchased or be acquired as part of a business combination. In either case, the treatment is capitalisation at cost or fair value under IFRS 3.

Bargain purchase

A **bargain purchase** arises when the fair value of the acquisition-date identifiable net assets acquired exceeds the consideration transferred.

- Before recognising a gain on bargain purchase, the acquirer must **reassess** whether it has correctly identified all the assets acquired and liabilities assumed
- Then the acquirer must **review the procedures** used to **measure** the amounts recognised for:
  - Identifiable net assets
  - Non-controlling interest (if any)
  - Interest previously held (if any)
  - Consideration transferred

Definition

Future economic benefits arising from assets that are not capable of being individually identified and separately recognised

- Recognise as an **asset** and measure at cost/excess of purchase cost over acquired interest
- Do **not amortise**
- Test at least annually for **impairment** (IAS 36)

You may be asked for a complicated calculation of goodwill as part of a group accounts question.

4: Employee benefits

Topic List

Short-term benefits

Retirement benefits

IAS 19 Employee benefits *is likely to be tested as part of a longer question rather than as a full question.*

IAS 19

IAS 19 *Employee benefits* deals with all employee benefits, not just pensions.

Objectives

An entity should recognise an expense as it consumes the economic benefits of employee service in exchange for employee benefits and a liability where these are to be paid in the future.

Examples – Short-term benefits

- Wages, salaries and social security contributions
- Paid annual/sick leave
- Profit sharing and bonuses (if payable within 12 months of year end)
- Non-monetary benefits (eg health care, accommodation etc)

Accounting treatment

- Recognise expense on an accruals basis (undiscounted)
- Short-term **accumulating** compensated absences (eg unused holiday carried forward) are recognised when the employee renders service increasing entitlement to compensated absences
- Short-term **non-accumulating** compensated absences (eg maternity pay) are recognised when the absences occur

Retirement benefits

Defined contribution plans are post-employment benefit plans under which an entity pays fixed contributions into a separate entity (a fund) and will have no legal or constructive obligation to pay further contributions if the fund does not hold sufficient assets to pay all employee benefits relating to employee service in current and prior periods.

Defined benefit plans are post-employment plans other than defined contribution plans.

Defined contribution plans

- The company's only obligation is to pay the agreed amount (normally a percentage of salary) into a plan on behalf of its employee
- *Accounting treatment:* charge contributions payable in respect of the accounting period; if amounts paid are different, then a prepayment/accrual will appear
- *Disclosure:* expense recognised for period

Defined benefit plans

- Role of actuary: calculates P/L charge for year; provides rate of expected return on assets and discount rate for liabilities (interest cost); values the assets and liabilities of pension fund, determines contributions required
- Accounted for by actuary measuring the liability using the projected unit credit method

Defined benefit plans

- The projected unit credit method sees each period of service as giving rise to an additional unit of benefit entitlement and measures each unit separateey to build up the final obligation

A suggested approach

Cost	*Recognise*
Interest cost on obligation	Increase in present value of defined benefit obligation because benefits are one year closer to payment. The discount rate is determined by reference to market yields on high quality fixed-rate corporate bonds. It is applied to the net defined benefit at the start of the accounting period. Debit Interest cost (x% × b/d obligation) (P/L) Credit PV defined benefit obligation (SOFP)

Interest on plan assets	Long-term expected increase in assets based on discount rate (determined as for interest cost on obligation) and applied to b/d assets. DEBIT Plan assets (SOFP) CREDIT Expected return (x% × b/d assets) (P/L) (Technically the expected return is also time apportioned on contributions less benefits paid in year)
Current service costs	Increase in the present value of defined benefit obligation as the result of employee service in the current period (provided by the actuary, but may need to be discounted back to period end). DEBIT Current service cost (P/L) CREDIT PV defined benefit obligation (SOFP)
Gains and losses on settlement	Difference between the value of the obligation being settled and the settlement price **Gain** DEBIT PV defined benefit obligation (SOFP) CREDIT Service cost (P/L) **Loss** DEBIT Service cost (P/L) CREDIT PV defined benefit obligation (SOFP)

Remeasurements: actuarial gains and losses	■ Arising from annual valuations of obligation ■ On obligation, differences between actuarial assumptions and actual experience during the period, or changes in actuarial assumptions **Gain** DEBIT PV defined benefit obligation (SOFP) CREDIT Other comprehensive income (SPLOCI) **Loss** DEBIT Other comprehensive income (SPLOCI) CREDIT PV defined benefit obligation (SOFP)
Remeasurements: return on assets	Arising from annual valuations of plan assets **Gain** DEBIT FV plan assets (SOFP) CREDIT Other comprehensive income (SPLOCI) **Loss** DEBIT Other comprehensive income (SPLOCI) CREDIT FV plan assets (SOFP)

Treatment of remeasurements (actuarial gain/loss)

IAS 19 requires actuarial gains and losses, now called remeasurements, to be recognised in the period incurred.

They are recognised in other comprehensive income and not reclassified (see Chapter 18) to profit or loss for the year.

Calculation of actuarial gain/loss

Market value of plan assets	$m
Market value of plan assets b/d	X
Interest on plan assets (x%)	X
Contributions	X
Benefits paid	(X)
Settlements	(X)
Return on plan assets: bal. figure	X
Market value of plan assets c/d	X

Present value of obligation	$m
PV of obligation at start of year	X
Interest cost (x%)	X
Current service cost	X
Past service cost	X
Benefits paid	(X)
Settlements	(X)
Actuarial (gain)/loss on obligation: bal. fig.	X
PV of obligation at end of year	X

5: Provisions, contingencies and EARP

Topic List

IAS 10

IAS 37

IASs 10 and 37 should both be familiar to you from your earlier studies. IAS 37 is particularly topical in the light of increasing environmental awareness. You may get asked about environmental liabilities as part of a disclosure question on the environmental report.

Events after the reporting period (EARPs)

Events, both favourable and unfavourable, which occur between the end of the reporting period and the date on which the financial statements are approved by the board of directors.

Adjusting events are EARPs which provide additional evidence of conditions existing at the reporting date, and therefore need to be incorporated into the financial statements. Non going-concern indicators after the reporting date are adjusting.

Non adjusting events are EARPs which concern conditions which did **not** exist at the reporting date. Do not adjust, but disclose if non-disclosure would affect the user's ability to make proper evaluations and decisions. Dividends proposed after reporting date: **do not** recognise as a liability.

Disclosure – for significant non-adjusting events: nature of the event, estimate of financial effect (or statement that estimate cannot be made).

IAS 37

IAS 37 *Provisions, contingent liabilities and contingent assets* was published in 1998 to remedy some abuses of provisions.

- Entities should **not provide** for **costs** that need to be incurred to **operate in the future,** if those **costs could be avoided** by the entity's future actions
- **Costs of restructuring** are to be recognised as a provision only when the entity has an **obligation** to carry out the restructuring
- The **full amount** of any **decommissioning costs** or environmental liabilities should be **recognised from the date on which they arise**

Provision

A liability of uncertain timing or amount. Liabilities are obligations to transfer economic benefits as a result of past transactions or events.

Contingent liability

Should be disclosed unless the possibility of any outflow of economic benefits to settle it is remote.

Contingent asset

Should be disclosed where an inflow of economic benefits is probable.

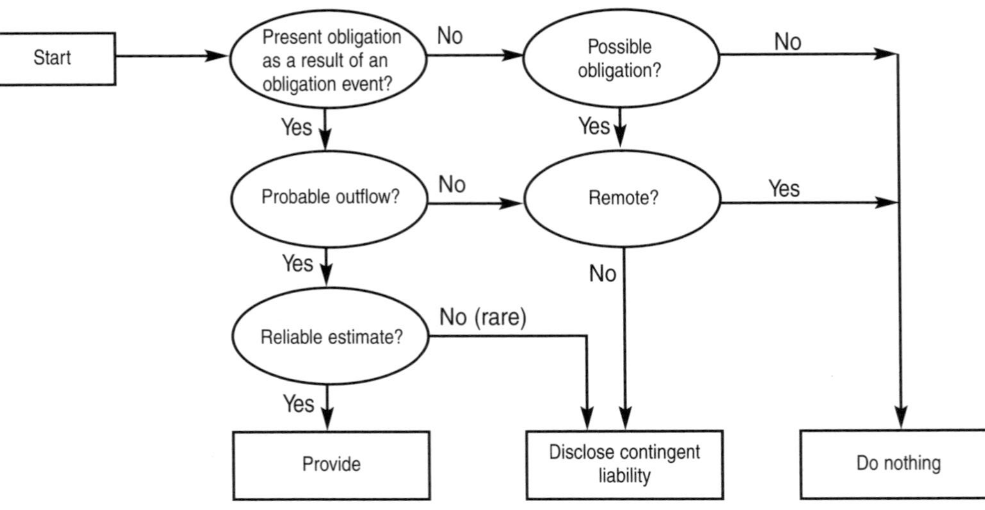
Start
Present obligation as a result of an obligation event?
No
Possible obligation?
No
Yes
Yes
Probable outflow?
No
Remote?
Yes
Yes
No
Reliable estimate?
No (rare)
Yes
Provide
Disclose contingent liability
Do nothing

6: Income taxes

Topic List

- IAS 12
- Deferred tax

IAS 12 on current tax is straightforward and should present no problems.

IAS 12 on deferred tax deals with the method of providing for deferred tax.

The December 2007, June 2010 and June 2012 paper had questions on deferred taxation.

IAS 12 requires the following treatment of *current tax*.

- Recognise a liability for amount unpaid, relating to current and prior periods
- Recognise an asset for amounts overpaid/tax losses

SPLOCI disclosure

Current tax	X
Under/(over) statement of prior periods	X
Deferred tax expense/(income) relating to	
– Origination and reversal of temporary differences	X
– Reduction in tax rate	(X)
Share of tax of associates	X
	X

SOFP disclosure

- Distinguish between current and deferred tax assets and liabilities
- Deferred tax assets/liabilities are based as non-current

Deferred tax

The tax charge to P/L is often different from tax rate times the profit before tax figure because of the differences which exist between tax rules and financial accounting principles.

Permanent differences arise where certain items in the I/S are either not taxable or not allowable.

Temporary differences arise where items are taxable/allowable but are dealt with in the tax computation in periods different from those in which they are included in the financial statements.

Basis of provision

- **Nil provision** – no provision
- **Full provision** – temporary differences provided for in full
- **Partial provision** – accounted for only to the extent that it is probable that a liability or asset will crystallise

Deferred tax is the tax attributable to temporary differences.

Examples

- Accelerated tax depreciation
- Intragroup profits in inventory
- Pension liabilities
- Revaluations
- Development costs
- Unrelieved tax losses
- Unremitted earnings of subsidiaries

Deferred tax is calculated by reference to the difference between the carrying value for accounts purposes and the tax base (value attributed for tax purposes).

Taxable temporary differences

Taxable temporary differences result in taxable profits in the future giving rise to a deferred tax liability

- Temporary differences where income or expense is included in accounting profit in one period and taxable profit in another are called **timing differences**
  - Interest revenue accrued for accounting purposes but taxed when received
  - Accelerated tax depreciation where tax (or 'capital') allowances are received at a rate higher than the accounting depreciation rate
  - Development costs which are a deferred expense for accounting purposes, but receive a tax deduction when paid
- Temporary differences also arise on:
  - Revaluations: the gain will be taxable in the future either on sale or if not sold by generating taxable income in excess of tax depreciation; the temporary difference is the estimated chargeable gain
  - Fair value adjustments: similar to revaluation but often occurring on consolidation

Deductible temporary differences

Deductible temporary differences result in tax deductible amounts in the future giving rise to a deferred tax asset.

- Examples are:
  - Accrued expenses/provisions which are not deducted for tax purposes until paid
  - Downward revaluations where no adjustment is made for tax purposes and hence the tax base exceeds carrying value

Alternative methods

- **Deferral method:** tax effects of temporary differences are calculated using tax rates current when differences arise
- **Liability method:** deferred tax liabilities are calculated at the rate at which it is estimated that tax will be paid (or recovered) when the temporary differences reverse

Accounting treatment

- Deferred tax is provided for under the full provision liability method but using tax rate enacted or substantially enacted at the balance sheet date
- Deferred tax assets and liabilities can only be offset if:
  - The entity has a legal right to set off current tax assets and liabilities, and
  - They relate to the same tax authority
- A deferred tax asset is recognised for unused tax losses/credits when it is probable that future taxable profit will be available to relieve them
- Deferred tax assets and liabilities should not be discounted

Disclosure

Statement of financial position

- Deferred tax asset/liability broken down by type of temporary difference
- Amount of current/deferred tax charged or credited directly to equity (eg revaluation)

SPLOCI

- Major components of the tax expense or income (see before)
- Explanation of relationship between tax expense and accounting profit, eg reconciliation of accounting profit × tax rate and tax expense identifying effect of temporary differences and/or changes in tax rate

7: Financial instruments

Topic List

Financial instruments

IAS 32

IFRS 9

IFRS 9 changes

IFRS 7

Fair value measurement

This is a controversial and complex topic. It is also the subject of recent significant change as IFRS 9 has replaced IAS 39.

The examiner is fond of this topic and has tested it at every sitting.

Relevant standards

IAS 32 deals with the classification of instruments as debt or equity.

IFRS 9 (July 2014) has replaced IAS 39 and deals with recognition, measurement, impairment and hedging.

IFRS 7 provides disclosure requirements for financial instruments.

Financial instrument

Any contract that gives rise to a financial asset of one entity and a financial liability or equity instrument of another.

Financial asset

Cash; equity instrument of another entity; contractual right to receive cash/other financial assets; contract that can be settled in the entity's own equity instruments and may be either a derivative or a non-derivative.

Financial liability

Contractual obligation to deliver cash/other financial asset; contractual obligation to exchange financial instruments under potentially unfavourable conditions.

Equity instrument

Contract that evidences a residual interest in the assets of an entity after deducting all its liabilities.

IAS 32 presentation

- Financial instruments should be classified as either
  - Liability (debt) or
  - Equity
- Compound instruments (exhibiting characteristics of both) must be split into their debt and equity components
- Substance rather than legal form applies (eg redeemable preference shares are a financial liability)
- Interest, dividends, loss or gains relating to a financial instrument classified as a liability are reported in the SPLOCI, while distributions to holders of equity instruments are debited directly to equity (in the SOCE)
- Offset of a financial asset and liability is only allowed where there is a legally enforceable right and the entity intends to settle net or simultaneously

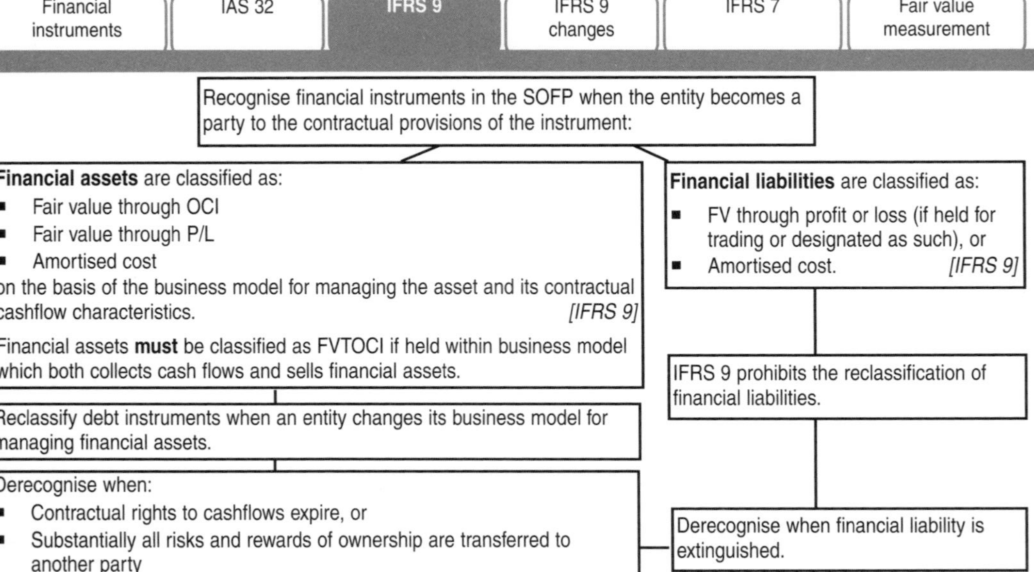

Recognise financial instruments in the SOFP when the entity becomes a party to the contractual provisions of the instrument:

Financial assets are classified as:

- Fair value through OCI
- Fair value through P/L
- Amortised cost

on the basis of the business model for managing the asset and its contractual cashflow characteristics. *[IFRS 9]*

Financial assets **must** be classified as FVTOCI if held within business model which both collects cash flows and sells financial assets.

Reclassify debt instruments when an entity changes its business model for managing financial assets.

Derecognise when:

- Contractual rights to cashflows expire, or
- Substantially all risks and rewards of ownership are transferred to another party

Financial liabilities are classified as:

- FV through profit or loss (if held for trading or designated as such), or
- Amortised cost. *[IFRS 9]*

IFRS 9 prohibits the reclassification of financial liabilities.

Derecognise when financial liability is extinguished.

	Initial measurement	Subsequent measurement	Related income/expense
Financial assets at amortised cost	FV of consideration given + transaction costs	Initial measurement - principal repayments +/- cumulative amortisation - impairments	Interest income (received + 'winding up') is recognised in profit or loss
Financial assets at fair value	FV of consideration given	Remeasured to FV at each period end	Changes in FV are recognised in – Profit or loss – OCI if business model achieved by collecting cash flows and selling financial assets – OCI if asset is equity instrument not held for trading and election made
Financial liabilities at amortised cost	FV of consideration received - transaction costs	Initial measurement - principal repayments +/- cumulative amortisation - impairments	Interest expense (paid + 'winding up') is recognised in profit or loss
Financial liabilities at FVTPL	FV of consideration received	Remeasured to FV at each period end	Changes in FV of financial liabilities held for trading are recognised in profit or loss

The change in FV of a financial liability DESIGNATED as FVTPL is split into two elements:

- Gain or loss from credit risk ⟶ recognise in OCI
- Other gain or loss ⟶ recognise in profit or loss

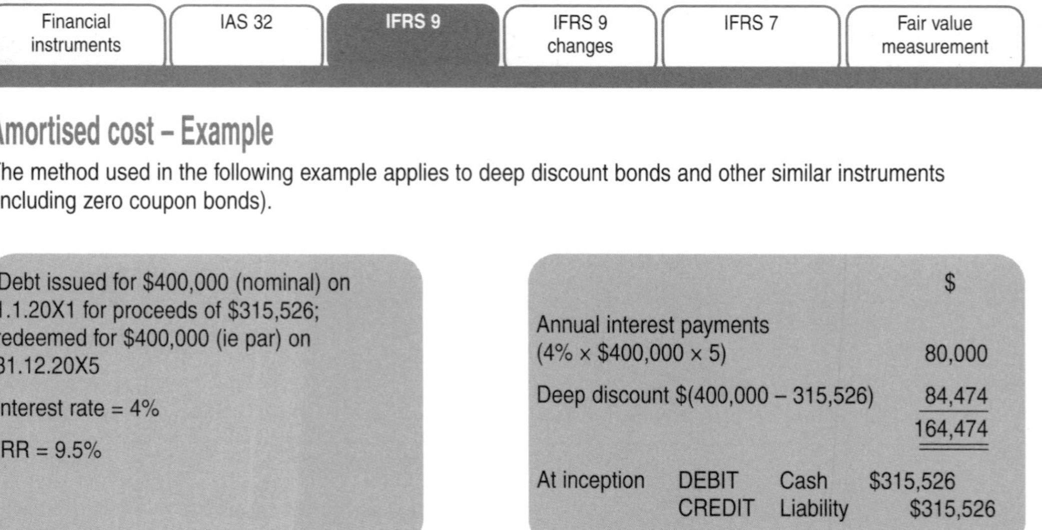

Amortised cost – Example

The method used in the following example applies to deep discount bonds and other similar instruments (including zero coupon bonds).

Debt issued for $400,000 (nominal) on 1.1.20X1 for proceeds of $315,526; redeemed for $400,000 (ie par) on 31.12.20X5

Interest rate = 4%

IRR = 9.5%

	$
Annual interest payments (4% × $400,000 × 5)	80,000
Deep discount $(400,000 – 315,526)	84,474
	164,474

At inception	DEBIT	Cash	$315,526
	CREDIT	Liability	$315,526

Year	P/L charge *$	Actual interest payable $	Winding up interest charged to P/L $	Liability in closing SOFP $
20X1	29,975	16,000	13,975	329,501
20X2	31,303	16,000	15,303	344,804
20X3	32,756	16,000	16,756	361,560
20X4	34,348	16,000	18,348	379,908
20X5	36,092	16,000	20,092	400,000
	164,474	80,000	84,474	

*9.5% x opening liability in SOFP

Fair value is measured as quoted market price in an active market where possible.

Overview

Impairment

- Impairment review where evidence of financial asset being impaired
- Expended credit loss model used
- Impairment loss is charged to P/L
- Where financial asset suffers impairment loss, cumulative losses on fair value adjustments previously recognised in equity are recycled in P/L as well as impairment loss
- Reversal: P/L

Embedded derivatives

= Derivatives embedded within a host contract, eg construction contract in foreign currency

HOST ≠ FINANCIAL ASSET
Separate derivative from host and account for as a derivative when conditions are met.
Account for host contract as normal, eg IAS 11

HOST = IFRS 9 FINANCIAL ASSET
Account for hybrid contract in accordance with IFRS 9

Hedging

Hedge accounting is mandatory where a transaction qualifies as a hedge (all criteria met):

- Economic relationship between the hedged item and the hedging instrument
- Effect of credt risk does not dominate value changes from the economic relationship
- Hedge ratio of hedging relationship is the same as that resulting from the quantity of the hedged item that the entity acutally hedges

IFRS 9 identifies three types of hedges which determines their accounting treatment.

Type	Hedges against	Accounting treatment
Fair value hedge	Changes in fair value of a recognised asset or liability or an unrecognised firm commitment* (or portion of either) that could affect profit or loss	■ Gain or loss on instrument is recognised in the P/L ■ Gain or loss on hedged item also recognised in P/L (and adjusts the carrying value of hedged item)
Cash flow hedge	Exposure to variability in cash flows attributable to a risk associated with a recognised asset or liability that could affect profit or loss	■ Gain or loss on effective portion of instrument is recognised in other comprehensive income (and recognised in P/L when asset or liability affects profit or loss, eg by interest income) ■ Gain or loss on ineffective portion is recognised in P/L
Hedge of net investment in a foreign operation	Variability in value of the net investment in a foreign operation or monetary items accounted for as part of that net investment	As for cash flow hedge

*IFRS 9 allows the hedge of a foreign currency firm commitment to be accounted for as a cash flow hedge.

IFRS 9 expected credit loss model

IFRS 9 used an **incurred loss model** for the impairment of financial assets. This assumed all loans will be repaid unless there is evidence to the contrary. This changed in the final version of IFRS 9 to an expected credit loss model.

- Effective interest rate to include an initial estimate of expected credit losses (therefore they are spread over instrument's life)
- Credit losses held in a separate allowance account (a reconciliation is disclosed)
- Losses due to changes in cash flow estimates disclosed as a separate line item
- 'Write-offs' direct to Financial Asset account if considered uncollectible
- Disclosures to show effect of credit losses, reconciliation of non-performing financial assets and results of any stress testing

Amount of impairment

The amount of the impairment to be recognised on these financial instruments **depends on whether or not they have significantly deteriorated** since their initial recognition.

Stage 1 Financial instruments whose credit quality has not significantly deteriorated since their initial recognition

Stage 2 Financial instruments whose credit quality has significantly deteriorated since their initial recognition

Stage 3 Financial instruments for which there is objective evidence of an impairment as at the reporting date

For stage 1 financial instruments, the impairment represents the present value of expected credit losses that will result if a default occurs in the 12 months after the reporting date **(12 months expected credit losses)**.

For financial instruments classified as stage 2 or 3, an impairment is recognised at the present value of expected credit shortfalls over their remaining life **(lifetime expected credit loss)**. Entities are required to reduce the gross carrying amount of a financial asset in the period in which they no longer have a reasonable expectation of recovery.

IFRS 9 Hedging changes

Under the final version of IFRS 9 the 80%-125% 'bright line' test of whether a hedging relationship qualifies for hedge accounting was replaced by an **objective-based assessment**:

- This allows genuine hedging relationships to be accounted for as such whereas the old IAS 39 rules sometimes **prevented** management from **accounting** for an actual hedging transaction as a hedge
- **Fair value hedges**: the IAS 39 treatment of recognising both changes in the fair value of the hedged item and changes in value of the hedging instrument in profit or loss is retained, but rules changed so that hedges of investments of equity instruments held at fair value through other comprehensive income can be accounted for as hedges
- **Cash flow hedges**: will continue to be accounted for as under IAS 39. Hedging gains and losses recognised in other comprehensive income will be recognised in a separate cash flow hedge reserve in equity

The main disclosures required are:

Statement of financial position

- Carrying amount of financial assets and liabilities by IFRS 9 category
- Reasons for any reclassification between fair value and amortised cost
- Details of assets and exposure to risk where transfers of assets have taken place
- Carrying amount of financial assets pledged as collateral
- Allowance for credit losses
- Multiple embedded derivatives
- Defaults and breaches

Statement of profit or loss and other comprehensive income

- Net gains/losses by IFRS 9 category
- Interest income/expense
- Impairment losses by class of financial asset

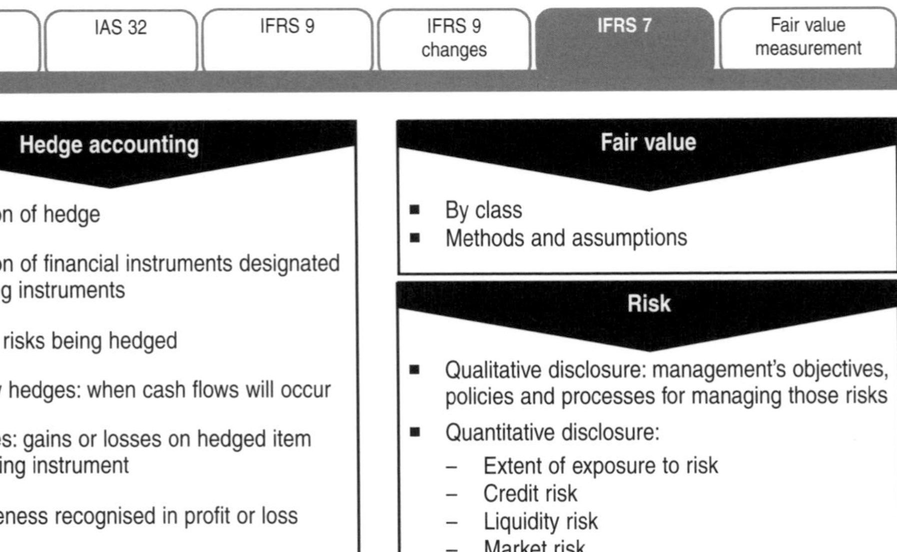
Hedge accounting
Description of hedge
Description of financial instruments designated as hedging instruments
Nature of risks being hedged
Cash flow hedges: when cash flows will occur
FV hedges: gains or losses on hedged item and hedging instrument
Ineffectiveness recognised in profit or loss
Fair value
By class
Methods and assumptions
Risk
Qualitative disclosure: management's objectives, policies and processes for managing those risks
Quantitative disclosure:
– Extent of exposure to risk
– Credit risk
– Liquidity risk
– Market risk

Fair value measurement

In May 2011 the IASB published IFRS 13 *Fair value measurement*. Its objective is to:

- Define fair value
- Set out in a single IFRS a framework for measuring fair value
- Require disclosure about fair value measurements

Fair value

The price that would be received to sell an asset or paid to transfer a liability in an orderly transaction between market participants at the measurement rate.

The rules of fair value measurement are brought together in IFRS 13 *Fair value measurement*.

IFRS 13

IFRS 13 states that valuation techniques must be those which are appropriate and for which sufficient data are available. Entities should maximise the use of relevant **observable inputs** and minimise the use of **unobservable inputs.**

The standard establishes a three-level hierarchy for the inputs that valuation techniques use to measure fair value:

Level 1 Quoted prices (unadjusted) in active markets for identical assets or liabilities that the reporting entity can access at the measurement date.

Level 2 Inputs other than quoted prices included within Level 1 that are observable for the asset or liability, either directly or indirectly, eg quoted prices for similar assets in active markets or for identical or similar assets in non active markets or use of quoted interest rates for valuation purposes.

Level 3 Unobservable inputs for the asset or liability, ie using the entity's own assumptions about market exit value.

8: Leases

Topic List

- Forms of lease
- Lessees
- Lessors
- Other issues
- Criticism of IAS 17

Leasing transactions are common in practice. The examiner is likely to test IAS 17 in conjunction with sale and leaseback transactions or revenue recognition aspects rather than the mechanics.

Finance lease

- Transfers substantially all the risks and rewards of ownership of an asset to the lessee; title may or may not be transferred
- Comparison of present value of minimum lease payments and fair value of leased asset is commonly used to judge whether risks and rewards have been transferred (no numerical guidance in IFRS)
- **PV:** calculate using the interest rate implicit in the lease
- Minimum lease payments are the payments over the lease term that the lessee is, or can be required to make (excluding contingent rent, costs for services and taxes to be paid by and reimbursed to the lessor), and
  - Lessee any amounts guaranteed by him or a party related to him
  - Lessor any residual value guaranteed to lessor by lessee, party related to lessee or independent third party
- **Lease term:** the period for which the lessee has contracted to lease the asset (primary **and** secondary periods)

Operating lease

A lease other than a finance lease

You should know this from your earlier studies.

Accounting treatment

- **Finance lease:** record as an asset and obligation at the lower of present value of the minimum lease payments and fair value
- The asset should be depreciated over the shorter of the lease term and its useful life
- A finance charge is made to produce a constant periodic rate of charge on the outstanding lease obligation (use actuarial method before tax and sum of the digits method)
- **Operating lease:** rentals charged on a straight-line basis over the lease term unless another systematic basis is representative of user's benefit

Disclosure

- Leased assets: net carrying amount at year end date
- Finance lease liabilities
  - Two disclosure notes
  - Reconciliation of minimum lease payments and PV
  - Breakdown of PV
  - For both, give maturity analysis (< 1 yr; 2-5 yrs; >5 yrs)
- Operating leases: future minimum lease payments under non-cancellable operating leases split < 1 yr, 2-5 yrs, > 5 yrs
- P/L (typical disclosures): depreciation charge on assets under finance leases, finance charge on finance leases, operating lease rentals, accounting policy

Lessors – accounting treatment

Finance lease

- Recognise receivable equal to net investment in the lease as a finance lease asset
- Mirror image of lessee's liability plus unguaranteed residual value
- Unguaranteed residual value is portion of residual value of asset not guaranteed by lessee or guaranteed only by party related to lessor
- Finance income recognised reflecting constant periodic rate of return on net investment outstanding

Operating lease

- Assets held for use under operating leases, are recorded as an asset on the SOFP and income in P/L on a straight line basis unless another systematic basis is more representative

You are unlikely to be asked for the disclosures for lessors.

Sales and leaseback transactions

- If leaseback is a **finance lease,** defer book profit/ loss and amortise over lease term

  Double entry is:

  DEBIT Cash
  CREDIT Finance lease liability

  and then as any other finance lease

- If leaseback transaction is an **operating lease;** where SP = sales proceeds; FV = fair value:
  - If SP = FV (see IFRS 13), recognise any profit/loss immediately
  - If SP < FV, recognise profit/loss immediately **unless** the apparent loss is compensated by future rentals at below market price, in which case defer and amortise
  - If SP > FV, defer the excess over FV and amortise over lease term (ie recognise FV minus Book Value)

Sale and leaseback transactions are a favourite with this examiner.

Criticisms of IAS 17

- IAS 17's key usefulness is the enforcing of application of 'economic substance over legal form'
- Without such enforcement leasing would be an example of off balance sheet financing
- No numerical guidance on what % of fair value constitutes a definite transfer of risks and rewards

ED leases

- Issued in May 2013 (original ED in 2010)
- The current IAS 17 **model of classification** of leases would **cease** to exist
- Lessees would **no longer be permitted to treat leases as 'off-balance sheet' financing,** but instead would be required to recognise an asset and liability for all leases within the scope of the proposed standard
- Options to extend a lease only included if there is a '**significant incentive**' to exercise them
- **Dual approach:**
  - For most real estate leases, report straight-line expense (like operating leases)
  - For other leases, approach similar to current finance leases

A leasing question may be connected to off balance sheet finance in general. In particular, you may be asked to discuss the links between IAS 17 and substance over form.

9: Share-based payment

Topic List

The issue

Types of transaction

The examiner tests this topic regularly., usually as part of a longer question. There was a full question on it in December 2010.

Share-based payments

Share-based payments are transactions whereby entities purchase goods and service from other parties, such as suppliers and employees, by issuing shares or share options.

The issue

This is a good example of substance over form. In the past when a limited liability company gave employees share options as remuneration, no expense was recognised in P/L.

This was believed to cause economic distortions and corporate governance concerns.

IFRS 2 deals with three types of share-based payment transactions.

- **Equity settled** share-based payment transactions: the entity receives goods or services as consideration for **equity instruments** or the entity (including shares or share options)
- **Cash-settled** share-based payment transactions: the entity acquires goods or services by incurring **liabilities** to the supplier of those goods and services for amounts that are based on the price (or value) of the entity's shares or other equity instruments

Recognition

DEBIT Expense (P/L)

CREDIT Equity (if equity-settled)

CREDIT Liability (if cash-settled)

- **Choice of equity/cash settled**: entity or supplier can choose whether to settle the transaction in cash or equity instruments

Measurement

Equity-settled

Use the fair value of goods received **OR**

If these cannot be measured reliably, measure indirectly by reference to the fair value of the equity instruments granted.

Estimating fair value of equity instruments:

- Shares: market price at **grant date**
- Share options: use **option pricing model** to estimate fair value at **grant date**

Cash-settled

Eg share appreciation rights. Employees become entitled to a future **cash payment based on** the **increase** in the entity's **share price**.

Company must **recognise** services received and related liability **as services are rendered**. Liability must be recognised at fair value using an option pricing model.

This fair value must be **updated at each year end.**

Choice

Entity has the choice: if there is a present obligation to settle in cash, treat as a cash-settled transaction. If not, treat as equity settled.

Counterparty has the choice: the entity has issued a compound financial instrument

- Treat debt component as cash settled
- Treat equity component as equity settled

10: Performance reporting

Topic List

- IASs 1 and 8
- IFRS 8 and IAS 33
- Ratio analysis
- Impact of changes
- Accounting theory and practice
- Management Commentary

You should be very familiar with IAS 8 from your earlier studies. However, it was tested in a challenging question on the December 2013 paper.

IFRS 8 deals with segment reporting.

EPS is less important than at earlier levels.

Ratio analysis is most likely to come up in the context of a change in accounting policy.

Accounting is open to manipulation. The Management Commentary may be useful in providing additional information.

IAS 1 *Presentation of financial statements* (revised 2011)

Prescribes format of statement of financial position, statement of profit or loss and other comprehensive income and statement of changes in equity (SOCIE).

- Identifies key accounting concepts:
  - Going concern
  - Accruals basis
  - Consistency of presentation
  - Materiality and aggregation
  - Offsetting (only when required/permitted by IFRS)
- All changes in equity arising from transactions with owners in their capacity as owners should be presented separately from non-owner changes in equity
- Income and expenses should be presented in one statement or in two
- Total comprehensive income to be presented in the financial statements

IAS 1 (revised 2011)

Key features of the 2011 revised IAS are:

- The performance statement is called the **statement of profit or loss and other comprehensive income**
- Entities are required to group items presented in other comprehensive income (OCI) on the basis of **whether they would be reclassified** to (recycled through) profit or loss at a later date, when specified conditions are met
- The amendment **does not address which items** are presented in other comprehensive income or which items need to be reclassified

XYZ Group – Statement of profit or loss and other comprehensive income

SINGLE STATEMENT

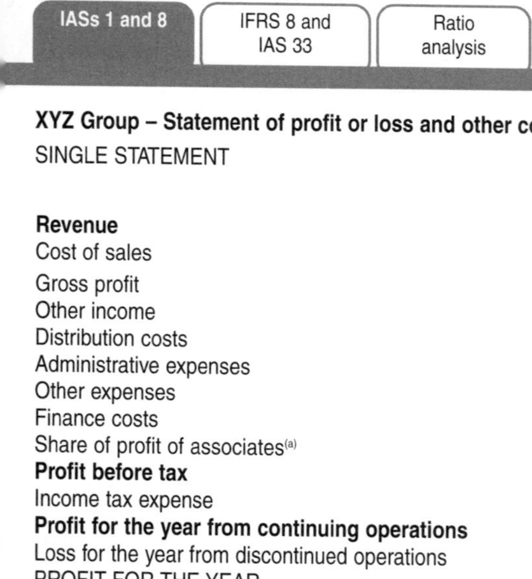

	20X7	*20X6*
Revenue	X	X
Cost of sales	(X)	(X)
Gross profit	X	X
Other income	X	(X)
Distribution costs	(X)	(X)
Administrative expenses	(X)	(X)
Other expenses	(X)	(X)
Finance costs	(X)	(X)
Share of profit of associates[a]	X	X
Profit before tax	X	X
Income tax expense	(X)	(X)
Profit for the year from continuing operations	X	X
Loss for the year from discontinued operations	X	(X)
PROFIT FOR THE YEAR	X	X

c/f

b/f		
Other comprehensive income:		
Items that will not be reclassified to profit or loss:		
Gains on property revaluation	X	X
Investment in equity instruments	(X)	X
Actuarial gains (losses) on defined benefit pension plans	(X)	X
Share of gain (loss) on property revaluation of associates	X	(X)
Income tax relating to items that will not be reclassifed	X	(X)
	(X)	X
Items that may be reclassified subsequently to profit or loss:		
Exchange differences on translating foreign operations	X	X
Cash flow hedges	(X)	(X)
Income tax relating to items that may be reclassified	(X)	(X)
	X	X
Other comprehensive income for the year, net of tax	(X)	X
TOTAL COMPREHENSIVE INCOME FOR THE YEAR	X	X

(a) This means the share of associates' profit attributable to owners of the associates, ie it is after tax and non-controlling interests in the associates.

(b) This illustrates the aggregated presentation, with disclosure of the current year gain or loss and reclassification adjustment presented in the notes. Alternatively, a gross presentation can be used.

(c) This means the share of associates' gain (loss) on property revalution attributable to owners of the associates, ie it is after tax and non-controlling interests in the associates.

(d) The income tax relating to each component of other comprehensive income is disclosed in the notes.

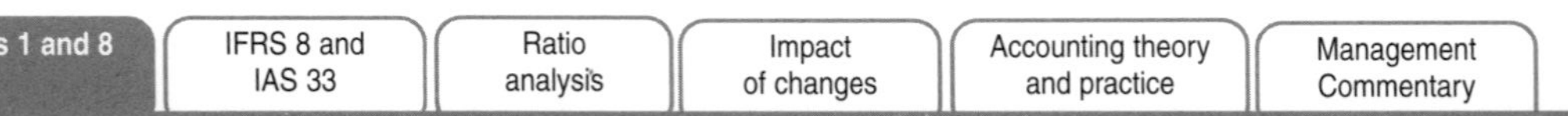

b/f		
Profit attributable to:		
Owners of the parent	X	X
Non-controlling interest	X	X
	X	X
Earnings per share (in currency units):		
Basic and diluted	X	(X)

(e) This means the share of associates' profit attributable to owners of the associates, ie it is after tax and non-controlling interests in the associates.

IAS 8

Should include all items of income and expense for the period (ie not hidden in reserves) unless an IFRS/IAS requires/permits otherwise.

Accounting policies

Accounting policies are the specific principles, bases, conventions, rules and practices applied by an entity in preparing and presenting statements.

An entity follows extant Standards and Interpretations when determining its accounting policies.

In the absence of a Standard or Interpretation covering a specific transaction, other event or condition, management uses its judgement to develop an accounting policy which results in information that is relevant and reliable, considering in the following order:

- Standards or Interpretations dealing with similar and related issues
- The *Conceptual Framework* definitions and recognition criteria
- Other national GAAPs based on a similar conceptual framework (providing the treatment does not conflict with extant Standards, Interpretations or the *Conceptual Framework*)

Changes in accounting policy

Only allowed if:

- Required by Standard or Interpretation
- If the change will provide more relevant or reliable information about events or transactions

Accounting treatment:

- Restate prior year SPLOCI and SOFP (Statement of Financial Position)
- Restate opening balance of retained earnings
- Include as second line of SOCIE
- Show effect on prior period at foot of prior year SPLOCI

Changes in accounting estimates

Apply **prospectively**, ie in the current period (and future periods if also affected).

Prior period errors

Omissions from and misstatements in the entity's financial statements for one or more periods.

Correct material prior period errors retrospectively in the first set of financial statements authorised for issue after their discovery.

- Restate comparative amounts for each prior period presented in which the error occurred
- Restate the opening balances of assets, liabilities and equity for the earliest prior period presented
- Include any adjustment to opening equity as the second line of the statement of changes in equity
- Disclose the nature of the error and the amount of the correction to prior periods for each line item in each period affected

Where it is impracticable to determine the period-specific effects or the cumulative effect of the error, the entity corrects the error from the earliest period/date practicable (and discloses that fact).

Reasons for segment information

- Explains factors which have contributed to company results
- Users can compare results of different products year/year
- Users can compare performance with competitors
- Users can assess future risks and rewards

IFRS 8 *Operating segments*

- **Segment reporting** is necessary for a better understanding and assessment of:
  - Past performance
  - Risks and returns
- IFRS 8 adopts the **managerial approach** to identifying segments
- The standard gives guidance on how segments should be **identified** and **what information should be disclosed** for each
- It also sets out requirements for related disclosures about **products and services, geographical areas and major customers**

IAS 33

EPS is a stock market indicator, so it is important that EPS is calculated on a comparable basis, year to year and company to company. *Drawback*: EPS relies on reported earnings; creative accounting can make a mockery of this.

IAS 33 applies to all entities whose ordinary shares or potential ordinary shares are publicly traded.

Basic calculation

$$\frac{\text{Net profit/loss attributable to ordinary shareholders}}{\text{Weighted average no. of shares outstanding during the period}}$$

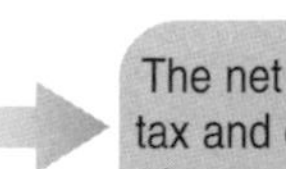

The net profit or loss used is after dividends, tax and deductions in respect of non-equity shares.

In an exam you are likely to meet EPS only in the context of the effects of different accounting treatments.

Information

User groups → Demand → Financial analysis

Sources:

- Published accounts/ interim statements
- Documents in Companies Register
- Government statistics
- Other published sources, eg Extel, Internet

Social/political considerations:

- *Social*. Fads? Green reporting. Employee information
- *Political*. Generally still self regulatory eg through SE
- *Multinational companies* have problems complying with different legislation/reporting requirements
- *Harmonisation* helps: EU directives, IASB

Stock exchange/efficient Market

Efficient market is one in which:

- Prices of shares reflect all relevant information available to buyers and sellers
- No individual dominates
- Transaction costs do not discourage trading

UK and US research suggests stockmarkets have semi-strong efficiency. Analysis carried out in the City helps create an efficient stock market. But what about Enron?

Profitability

Return on capital employed

$$ROCE = \frac{PBIT}{\text{Capital employed}} = \frac{PBIT}{\text{Total assets less current liabilities}}$$

Return on equity

$$ROE = \frac{\text{Profit after tax and pref div}}{\text{Ord share capital + reserves}} \%$$

More restricted view of capital than ROCE, but same principles.

When interpreting look for the following:

- How risky is the business?
- How capital intensive?
- What ROCE do similar business have?

Problems: comparability

- Revaluation reserves
- Policies, eg depreciation, R&D
- Bank overdraft: short/ long-term liability
- Investments and related income: exclude

Profit margin

Asset turnover

You should know these!

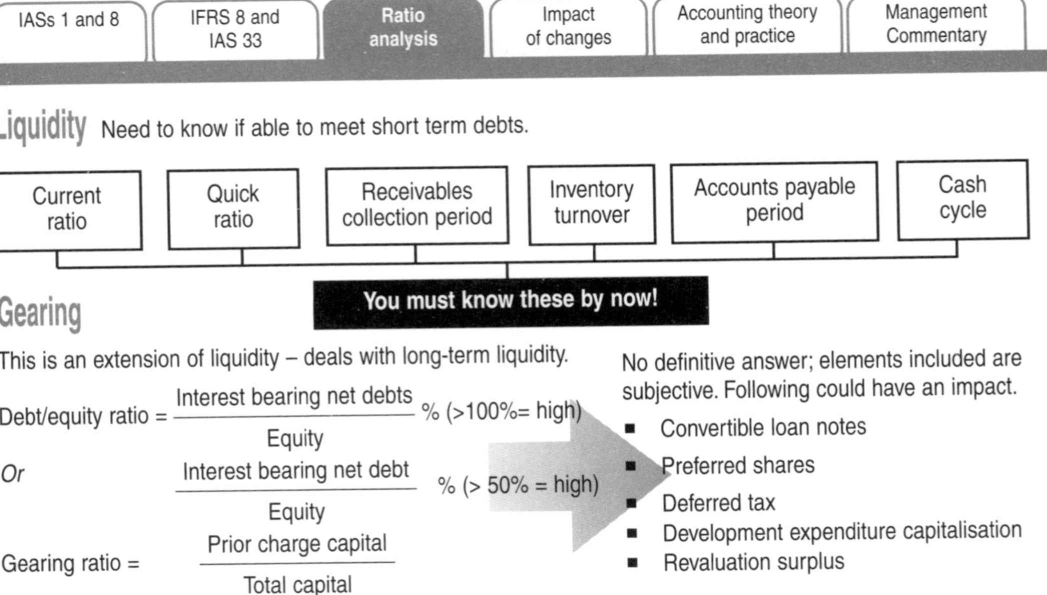

Liquidity

Need to know if able to meet short term debts.

Gearing

This is an extension of liquidity – deals with long-term liquidity.

$$\text{Debt/equity ratio} = \frac{\text{Interest bearing net debts}}{\text{Equity}}\ \% \ (>100\% = \text{high})$$

Or

$$\frac{\text{Interest bearing net debt}}{\text{Equity}}\ \% \ (>50\% = \text{high})$$

$$\text{Gearing ratio} = \frac{\text{Prior charge capital}}{\text{Total capital}}$$

No definitive answer; elements included are subjective. Following could have an impact.

- Convertible loan notes
- Preferred shares
- Deferred tax
- Development expenditure capitalisation
- Revaluation surplus

Investors' ratios

Used by someone contemplating investment. Consider a company's shares as a source of income (dividends) and/or source of capital growth (share price).

Dividend yield

$$\text{Dividend yield} = \frac{\text{Div per share}}{\text{Mid-market price}} \%$$

- *Low yield:* retains a large proportion of profits to reinvest
- *High yield:* risky company **or** slow-growing

Dividend cover

$$\text{Dividend cover} = \frac{\text{EPS}}{\text{Div per share}}$$

or

$$\frac{\text{Profit after tax and pref div}}{\text{Div on ordinary shares}}$$

Shows how safe the dividend is, or extent of profit retention. Variations due to maintaining dividend vs declining profits

P/E ratio

$$\text{P/E ratio} = \frac{\text{Mid-market price}}{\text{EPS}}$$

Higher the better; reflects confidence of market; rise in EPS will cause rise in P/E ratio, but maybe not to same extent

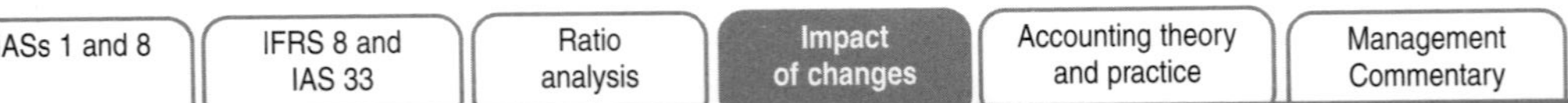

Changes in accounting policy

- Can be a chance for manipulation
- Less so now choices are being eliminated

Changes in accounting standards

- Can be far reaching
- Eg revision of IFRS 3

Change and the P2 exam

- Likely to be tested
- You will be required to advise the director about the impact of a change
- Alternatively, you will need to correct an accounting treatment that is wrong

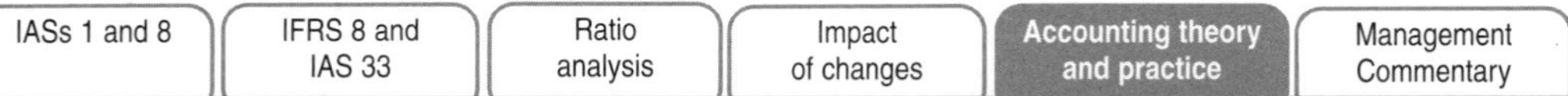

Limitations of financial analysis

Here is a summary of the limitations of financial analysis.

- Availability of comparable information
- Use of historical/out-of-date information
- Ratios are not definitive – they are only a guide
- Needs careful analysis; do not consider in isolation
- It is a subjective exercise
- It can be subject to manipulation
- Ratios are not defined in standard form

Limitations of accounting data

- Profit is subjective and may be manipulated by choice of accounting policy
- Seasonal fluctuations
- Window dressing

In the UK, companies are encouraged to produce an Operating and Financial Review, analysing a company's financial position and performance. A Practice Statement *Management Commentary* gives guidance on an international equivalent. Given the limitations of accounts, this review should prove useful.

Purpose

- Interpret financial statements in the context of the **entity's operating environment**
- Assess what **management** views as the **most important issues**
- Assess the **strategies** adopted by the entity and their likelihood of success

Contents

- Should **supplement and complement** the financial statements
- Should be from the **management's perspective**
- Should have an orientation towards the **future**
- Should be
  - understandable
  - relevant
  - balanced
  - comparable over time

11: Related parties

Topic List

Related party disclosures

This topic is new to you at P2, and so could well be tested, either as a full question or part of a question.

Key elements: control, joint control, significant influence

A **person** is related to an entity if:

(1) They control or jointly control the entity (Mr A & B)
(2) They have significant influence over the entity (Mr A & C)
(3) They are key management personnel of the entity or its parent
(4) They are a close family member of any individual in (1)-(3)

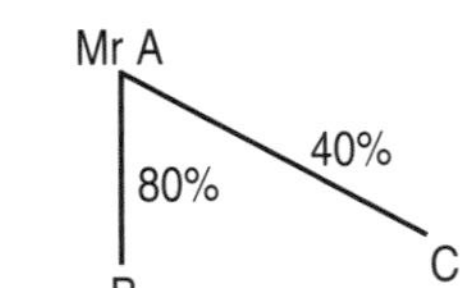

PLUS where an individual controls/jointly controls/has significant influence over two entities, they are related

An **entity** is related to another entity if:

(1) They are members of the same group (Z & Y)
(2) One is an associate or JV of the other (Z & X)
(3) Both are JVs of a third party (W & U)
(4) One is an associate and the other a JV of a third party (X & W)
(5) One is a pension plan for employees of the other

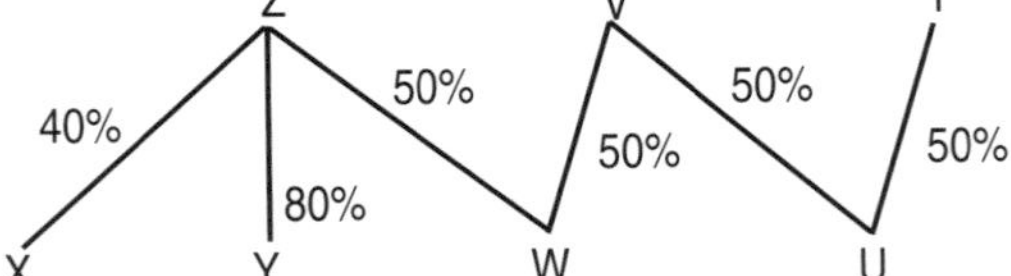

KEY FACTOR: SUBSTANCE OF RELATIONSHIP

Not necessarily related parties

- Two entities simply because they have a director in common
- Two venturers simply because they share joint control of a joint venture
- Providers of finance, trade unions, public utilities, government departments and agencies in the course of their normal dealings with an entity by virtue only of those dealings
- A single customer, supplier, franchisor, distributor or general agent with whom an entity transacts a significant volume of business merely by virtue of the resulting economic dependence

Disclosure

Always

(1) Name of parent + ultimate controlling party

(2) Key management personnel compensation

Where RP transactions have occurred disclose for each category of related party

(1) Nature of relationship

(2) Amount of transactions

(3) Amount of outstanding balances

(4) Provision for doubtful debts

(5) Bad debt expense re related parties

Notes

12: Revision of basic groups

Topic List

- Group accounts
- IFRS 10 *Consolidated financial statements*
- IFRS 3 *Business combinations*
- Summary of technique
- Associates and joint ventures
- IFRS 12 *Disclosure of interests in other entities*

Some of this chapter should be very familiar to you. However, IFRS 11 on joint arrangements is new.

You will always get a compulsory groups question in the exam. It will be part of a longer case study for 50 marks.

You have met associates but not joint arrangements in your earlier studies.

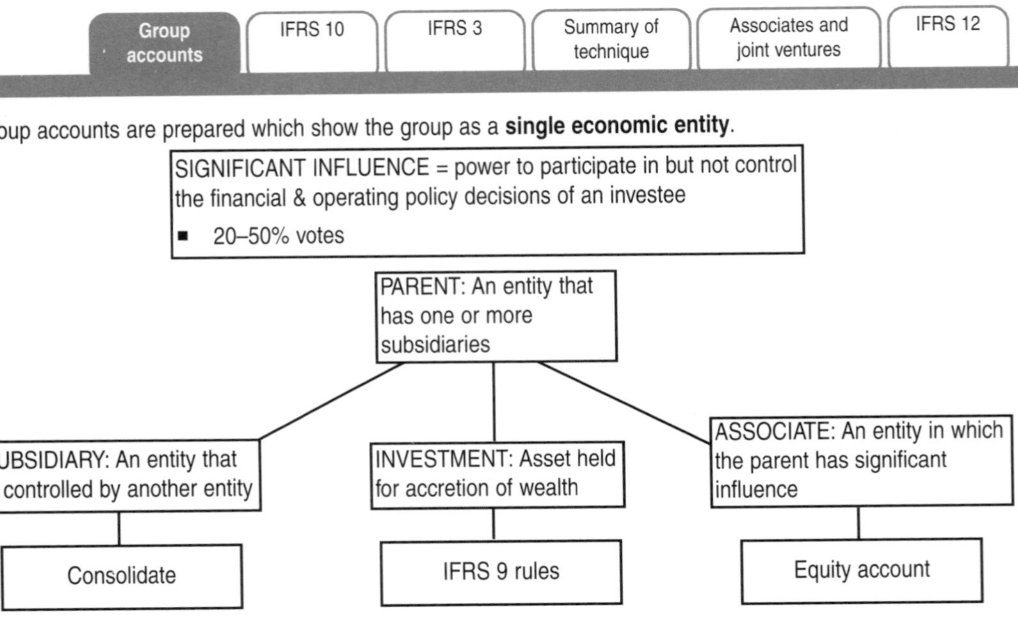
Group accounts are prepared which show the group as a **single economic entity**.
SIGNIFICANT INFLUENCE = power to participate in but not control the financial & operating policy decisions of an investee
■ 20–50% votes
PARENT: An entity that has one or more subsidiaries
SUBSIDIARY: An entity that is controlled by another entity
INVESTMENT: Asset held for accretion of wealth
ASSOCIATE: An entity in which the parent has significant influence
Consolidate
IFRS 9 rules
Equity account

Control

An investor controls an investee if it has:

- Power over the investee
- Exposure or rights to variable returns from involvement with the investee
- The ability to use its power over the investee to affect the amount of returns it receives

Power

Existing rights that give the current ability to direct the relevant activities of the investee.

Power may be achieved through holding a majority of voting rights or by other means.

Returns

May include:

- Dividends
- Remuneration for servicing investee's assets and liabilties
- Fees and exposure to loss from the provision of credit support

Consolidated financial statements

Consolidated financial statements include all subsidiaries other than those held for sale or those which operate under long term restrictions and so are not controlled.

Exemption

A parent need not prepare group accounts if:

- It is itself a wholly owned subsidiary
- It is partially owned and the other owners do not object
- Its securities are not publicly traded
- The ultimate or intermediate parent publishes IFRS-compliant consolidated accounts
- Disclosures apply

Preparation

- Different reporting dates – adjustments should be made
- Uniform accounting policies – if not, disclose why. Adjustments should be made on consolidation
- Intra-group transactions are eliminated

Parent's accounts

Subsidiaries are accounted for at cost or in accordance with IFRS 9

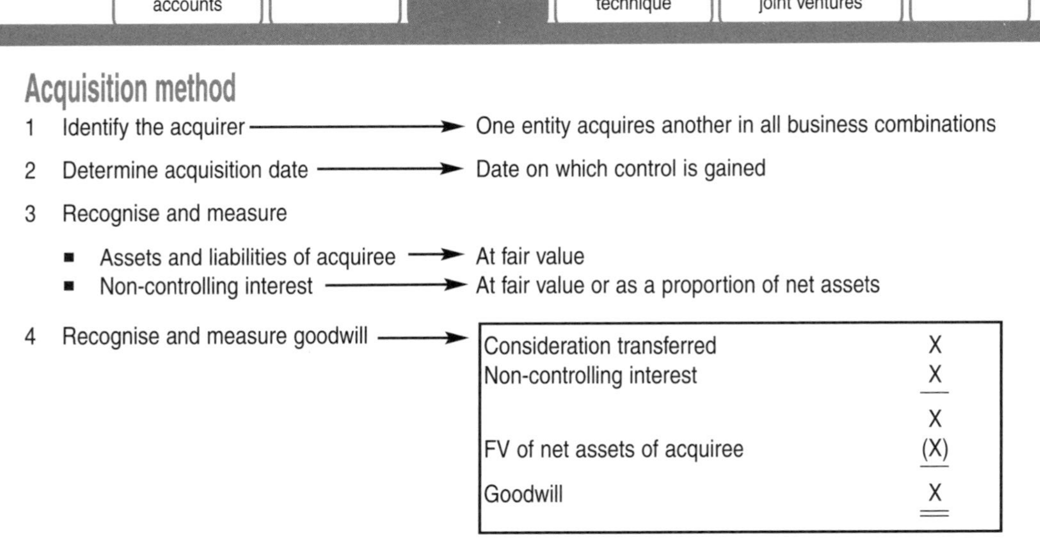

Acquisition method

1 Identify the acquirer → One entity acquires another in all business combinations

2 Determine acquisition date → Date on which control is gained

3 Recognise and measure

- Assets and liabilities of acquiree → At fair value
- Non-controlling interest → At fair value or as a proportion of net assets

4 Recognise and measure goodwill →

Consideration transferred	X
Non-controlling interest	X
	X
FV of net assets of acquiree	(X)
Goodwill	X

CONSIDERATION TRANSFERRED

- Cash/other assets
- Shares
- Debt instruments
  - Record contingent consideration at fair value
  - Exclude consideration relating to pre-existing relationships
  - Exclude acquisition costs (which are expensed)

NON-CONTROLLING INTEREST

Measure at:

- Fair value, or
- As proportion of net assets

Fair value should be determined based on market value of shares or valuation techniques. It is not extrapolated from consideration transferred for controlling interest. If the NCI is not entitled to a proportionate share of net assets on a winding up, the NCI must be measured at FV.

When fair value is used to measure the NCI, goodwill represents all of the goodwill of the business, not just the parent's share.

FV OF NET ASSETS ACQUIRED

All assets and liabilities are included at fair value in accordance with IFRS 13 (Ch 7)

- Exclude liabilities for future losses
- Include identifiable intangible assets
- Include contingent liabilities if fair value can be measured reliably
- Include reacquired rights & indemnification assets
- Use relevant standards to measure deferred tax, pensions, share-based payments & assets held for sale

Disclosures

- Name and description of acquiree and date of acquisition
- Share of voting rights acquired and reason for combination
- Description of factors making up goodwill
- Consideration transferred by type and details of contingent consideration
- Details of assets and liabilities acquired
- The gain in a bargain purchase and a description of why it arose
- The NCI and measurement basis applied plus details of techniques to determine fair value where relevant

Fair values

On consolidation, the **fair value** of the consideration paid for a subsidiary is compared with the **fair value** of the identifiable assets and liabilities acquired. Fair value is determined in accordance with IFRS 13, which was covered in Chapter 7.

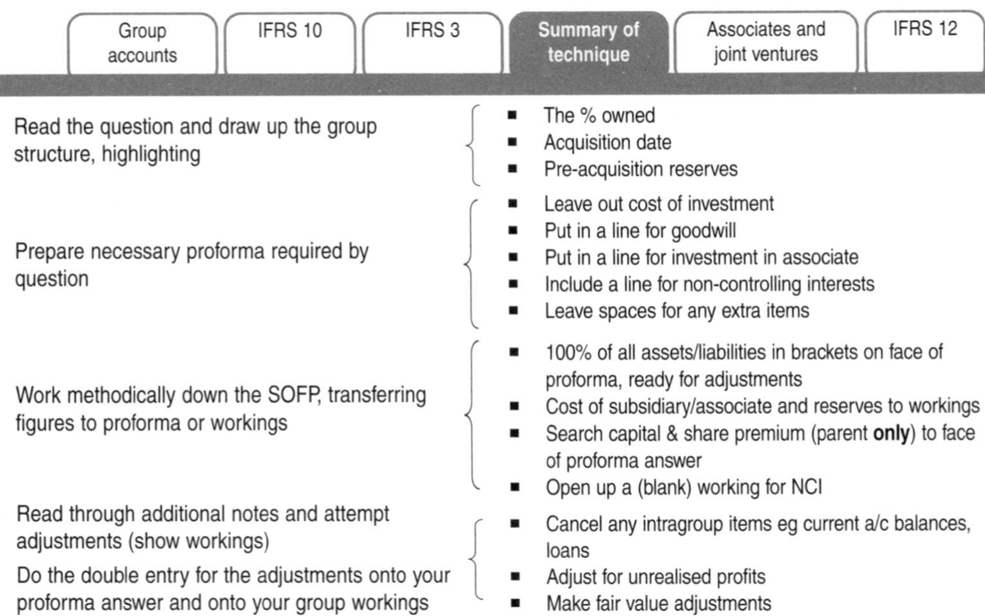

1 Read the question and draw up the group structure, highlighting	■ The % owned ■ Acquisition date ■ Pre-acquisition reserves
2 Prepare necessary proforma required by question	■ Leave out cost of investment ■ Put in a line for goodwill ■ Put in a line for investment in associate ■ Include a line for non-controlling interests ■ Leave spaces for any extra items
3 Work methodically down the SOFP, transferring figures to proforma or workings	■ 100% of all assets/liabilities in brackets on face of proforma, ready for adjustments ■ Cost of subsidiary/associate and reserves to workings ■ Search capital & share premium (parent **only**) to face of proforma answer ■ Open up a (blank) working for NCI
4 Read through additional notes and attempt adjustments (show workings) Do the double entry for the adjustments onto your proforma answer and onto your group workings	■ Cancel any intragroup items eg current a/c balances, loans ■ Adjust for unrealised profits ■ Make fair value adjustments

5 Complete goodwill calculation

Consideration transferred		X
Non-controlling interest		X
Net assets acquired as represented by		
Share capital	X	
Share premium	X	
Other reserves at acquisition	X	
Retained earnings at acquisition	X	
Fair value adjustments	X	
		(X)
Goodwill		X
Less impairment losses to date		(X)
		X

The NCI at acquisition will be either at % FV of net assets **or** at full FV

6 Complete retained earnings calculation

	P	S	A
Per question	X	X	X
Adjustments	X/(X)	X/(X)	X/(X)
	X	Y	Z
Share of subsidiary post acquisition (Y × %)	X		
Share of associate post acquisition (Z × %)	X		
	X		
Any impairment of goodwill	(X)		
	X		

Note – A similar working is used for any other reserves

7 Complete 'Investment in associate' (if appropriate):

Cost of associate	X
Share of post-acquisition retained reserves (from reserves working)	X
Less group impairment losses on associate to date	(X)
	X

8 Complete non-controlling interest calculation

NCI at acquisition	X
NCI share of post acq'n reserves	X
Loss: NCI share of impairment losses (**only if NCI at full FV at acq'n**)	(X)
	X

Workings for common adjustments

Calculation of provision for unrealised profit

Unrealised profit on intragroup sales	X		
% held @ y/e	%		
= Provision for unrealised profit (PUP)	X	DR	Retained earnings
(adjust in company **selling** goods)		CR	Group inventories

Calculation of fair value adjustments

	Acq'n date	*Movement*	*Year end*	
Inventories	X	(X)	X	Adjust figures in SOFP
Depreciable non-current assets	X	(X)	X	
Non-depreciable non-current assets	X	(X)	X	
Other fair value adjustments	X/(X)	X/(X)	X/(X)	
	X	X	X	
	↓ Goodwill	↓ Ret'd earnings		

IAS 28 *Associates and joint ventures*

Significant influence

Presumed when 20%–50% voting shares are held

Evidenced by:

- Board representation
- Participation in policy making
- Material transactions between investor and investee
- Interchange of management personnel
- Provision of essential technical information

Equity method

Method of accounting for an associate or joint venture. Applied where consolidated accounts are prepared, ie the parent also has a subsidiary. Also, where an investor has an associate but no subsidiaries, then the investor does not prepare consolidated accounts, but includes the associate in its own accounts using the equity method.

An ED *Equity method: share of other net asset changes* (November 2012) provides additional guidance on how investors should recognise their share of changes in the net assets of an investee that are not recognised in P/L or OCI and are not distributions. Investors should recognise their share of such changes in the investors' equity.

The criteria that exist to identify a joint venture are covered in Chapter 13.

Consolidated statement of financial position – equity method

Investment in associate

	$
Cost of investment	X
Add share of post-acquisition reserves	X
Less impairment losses to date	(X)
	X

Consolidated statement of profit or loss and other comprehensive income

- Share of profit after tax
- Share of other comprehensive income

Adjustments

- Transactions between the group and the associate are not eliminated
- **Group share** of unrealised profits is eliminated
  - Against inventories (where associate is seller)
  - Against investment (where parent is seller)
- Excess depreciation on FV adjustments

Exception: use IFRS 5 if investment acquired and held for sale.

IFRS 12 *Disclosure of interests in other entities*

Disclose:

- Significant judgements and assumptions made in determining the nature of an interest in another entity
- Information about subsidiaries, associates, joint arrangements and structures entities that are not controlled by an entity

Disclosure of subsidiaries

- Interests of NCI in group activities and cash flows
- The nature and extent of restrictions of investor's ability to use group assets and liabilities
- The nature of risks associated with interests in consolidated structured entities
- Consequences of changes in ownership interest

Disclosure of associates / joint arrangements

- The nature, extent and financial effects of an entity's interests in associates or joint arrangements
- Risks associated with an interest in an associate or joint arrangement

13: Complex groups and joint arrangements

Topic List

- Complex groups
- Sub-subsidiaries
- 'D' shaped groups
- Joint arrangements

This chapter covers one of the more complicated consolidation topics that you meet for the first time at Paper P2.

It is always helpful to sketch a diagram of the group structure.

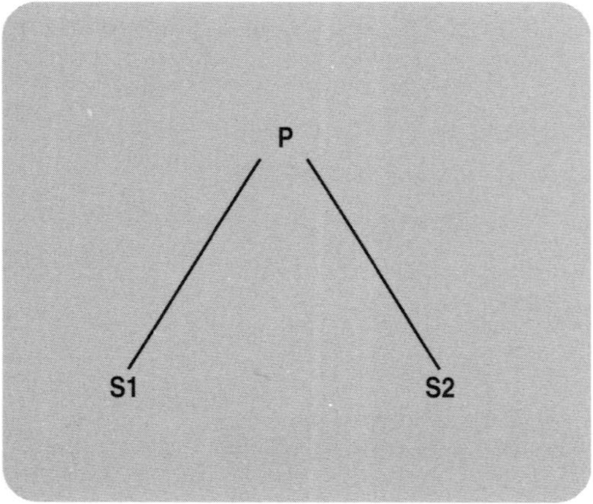

P

S1 S2

Several subsidiary entities

In the consolidated statement of financial position:

- A single figure is given for non-controlling interest
- Separate totals for goodwill and gain on a bargain purchase arising

P **controls** S

S **controls** SS

Therefore P **controls** SS

P effectively **owns** (80% × 80%) 64% of SS

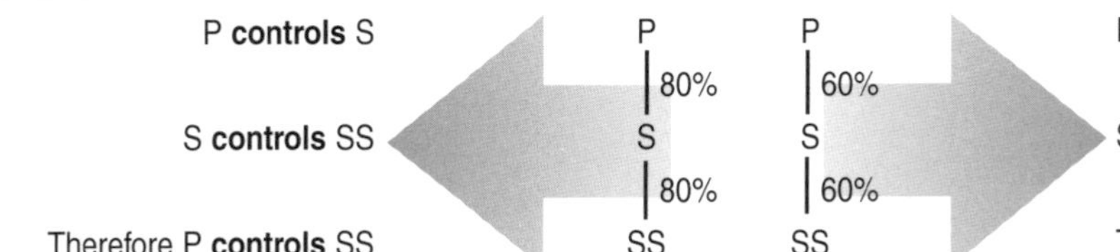

P **controls** S

S **controls** SS

Therefore P **controls** SS

P effectively **owns** (60% × 60%) 36% of SS

Consolidation method:

Net assets: show what group **controls.**

Capital and reserves: based on **effective holdings** eg 80% × 80% = 64% therefore NCI = 100% – 64% = 36%.

Date of effective control:

SS comes under P's control:

- Date S acquired, if S already holds shares in SS
- If S acquired SS later, that later date

Exam focus point

You must identify subsidiaries based on **control**. Then most of the consolidation is the same as for a simple group.

A complex group structure has an impact on two of the basic workings you need for a consolidated statement of financial position

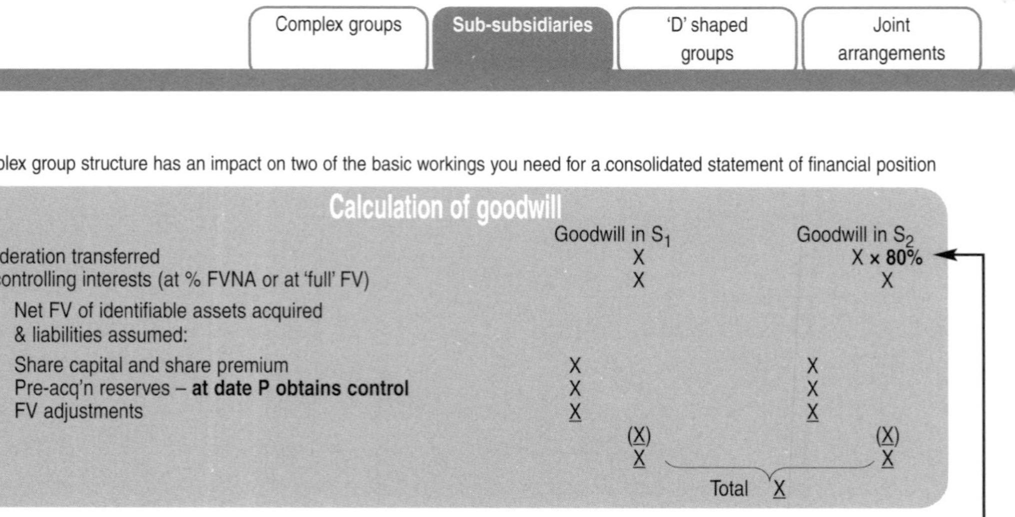

Calculation of goodwill

	Goodwill in S_1		Goodwill in S_2	
Consideration transferred		X		X × **80%**
Non-controlling interests (at % FVNA or at 'full' FV)		X		X
Less: Net FV of identifiable assets acquired & liabilities assumed:				
Share capital and share premium	X		X	
Pre-acq'n reserves – **at date P obtains control**	X		X	
FV adjustments	X		X	
		(X)		(X)
		X		X
Total			X	

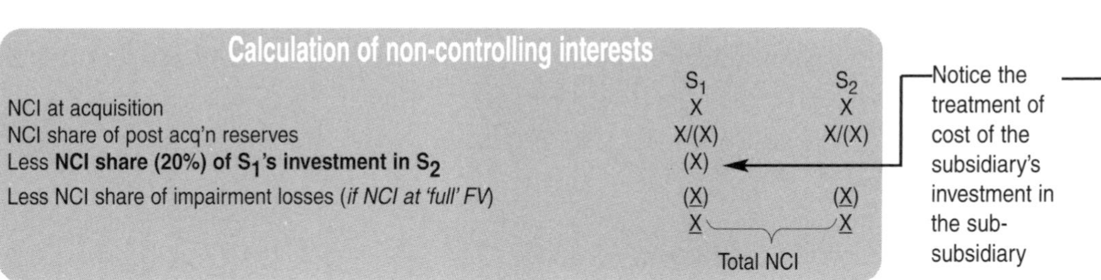

Calculation of non-controlling interests

	S_1	S_2
NCI at acquisition	X	X
NCI share of post acq'n reserves	X/(X)	X/(X)
Less **NCI share (20%) of S_1's investment in S_2**	(X)	
Less NCI share of impairment losses (*if NCI at 'full' FV*)	(X)	(X)
	X	X
	Total NCI	

Notice the treatment of cost of the subsidiary's investment in the sub-subsidiary

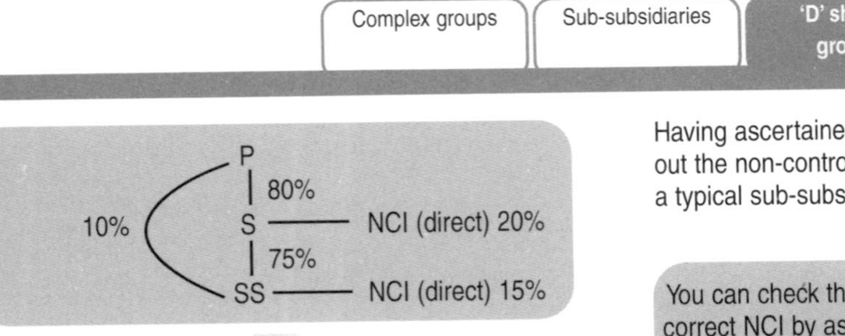

In this structure there is

■ A direct NCI in S of		20%
■ A direct NCI in SS of	15%	
■ An indirect NCI in SS of 20% × 75%	15%	
		30%

Having ascertained the structure and worked out the non-controlling interests, proceed as for a typical sub-subsidiary situation.

You can check that you have worked out the correct NCI by assuming a dividend distribution of $100 from SS.

S will receive $75

P will receive 80% × $75	60
P will receive 10% × $100	10
	70
Leaving for NCI in SS	30

IFRS 11 *Joint arrangements*

IFRS 11 was published in 2011. It defines a joint arrangement and provides criteria for distinguishing between joint ventures and joint operations.

Joint control

The contractually agreed sharing of control which exists when decisions about relevant activities require unanimous consent of the parties sharing control.

Joint arrangement

An arrangement in which two or more parties have joint control.

Joint operations

Parties with joint control have rights to the assets and obligations for the liabilities of the joint arrangement.

Includes all joint arrangements not structured through a separate entity.

Joint ventures

Parties with joint control have rights to the net assets of the arrangement.

Accounting for joint arrangements

Joint operation

Joint operator should recognise:

- Its assets including its share of jointly-held assets
- Its liabilities including its share of jointly-incurred liabilities
- Revenue from the sale of its share of output from the joint operation
- Its share of revenue from the sale of output by the joint operation
- Its expenses including its share of expenses incurred jointly

Joint venture

A joint venturer should recognise its interest in a joint venture as an investment and account for that investment using the equity method (IAS 28). This was covered in Chapter 12 and is the same as for associates.

An ED was issued in 2012 giving guidance on accounting for acquisitions of interests in joint operations – acquirers should apply the principles in IFRS 3 and other relevant standards.

Another 2012 ED, **sale or contribution of assets between an investor and its associate or joint venture**, addresses discrepancies between IAS 28 and IFRS 10.

14: Changes in group structures

Topic List

- Disposals
- Business combinations achieved in stages
- Changes in direct ownership

Don't be afraid of the topics in this chapter, they are all within your grasp, provided a logical approach is adopted.

Question practice is crucial.

Gain or loss on disposal is calculated as follows.

In parent company

	$
FV of consideration received	X
Less carrying value of investment	(X)
Profit/(loss)	X/(X)

The treatment in the group accounts depends on whether control is lost (ie whether the 50% boundary is crossed).

In group accounts where control is lost

	$
FV of consideration received	X
FV of investment retained	X
Less net assets x share (%) held at date control lost	(X)
Less goodwill	(X)
Group profit (loss)	X/(X)

In group accounts (control retained)

	$
FV of consideration received	X
Increase in NCI in net assets at disposal	(X)
	X

No gain or loss is recognised. This total is shown as an adjustment to the equity owned by the parent.

Full disposal

- In SPLOCI
  - Consolidated results to date of disposal
  - Show group gain or loss separately before interest
- In SOFP: no subsidiary therefore no consolidation or NCI

Subsidiary to subsidiary

- NCI in SPLOCI will be based on % before and after disposal, ie time apportion
- No group gain or loss as control retained
- NCI in SOFP based on year end %
- Adjustment to parent's equity will be made between NCI and retained earnings in SOFP

Subsidiary to associate

- SPLOCI: treat as subsidiary to date of disposal, consolidate for correct no. of months and show NCI in that amount. Treat as associate thereafter
- SOFP: Fair value at date of disposal; equity account thereafter

Subsidiary to trade investment

- SPLOCI: treat as subsidiary to date of disposal. Show dividend income only thereafter
- SOFP: Fair value of remaining investment at date of disposal; available for sale investment (IFRS 9) thereafter

A controlling interest in a subsidiary may be built up over a period of time. The important point is when **control is obtained,** which is usually when the **50% threshold is crossed**.

Associate becomes subsidiary

Consideration transferred		X
FV of associate		X
Less FV identifiable net assets	X	
Group share %		(X)
Goodwill		X

Increase in control eg 60% sub to 80% sub

Fair value of consideration paid	(X)
Decrease in NCI at date of transaction	(X)
Adjustment to parent equity	(X)

Reasons for group reorganisation

- A group may want to float a business to **reduce the gearing** of the group. The holding company will initially transfer the business into a separate company
- Companies may be transferred to another business during a **divisionalisation** process
- The group may 'reverse' into another company to obtain a **stock exchange quotation**
- Internal reorganisations may create efficiencies of group structure for **tax purposes**

New top holding company

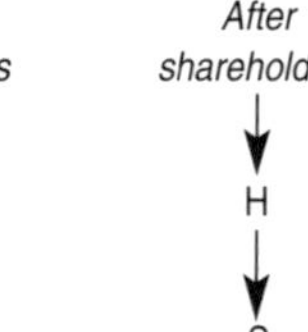

Subsidiary moved up

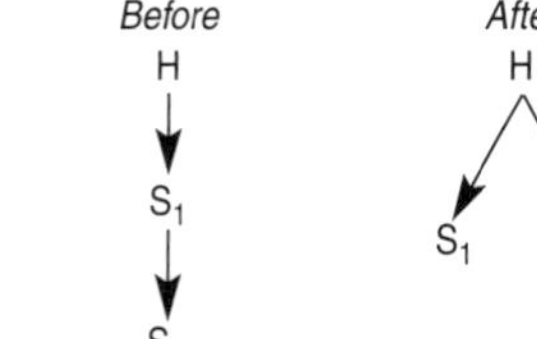

Subsidiary moved along

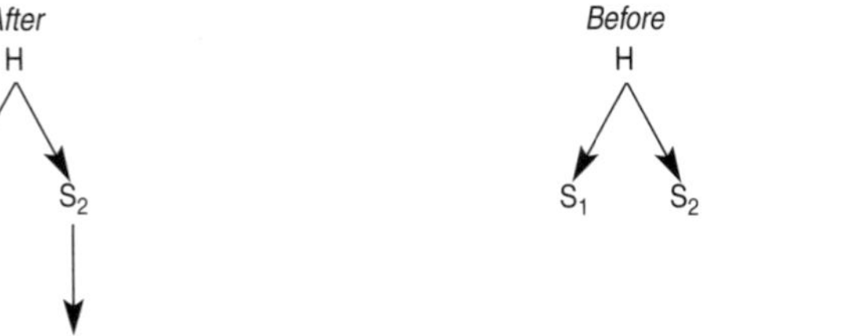

Subsidiary moved down

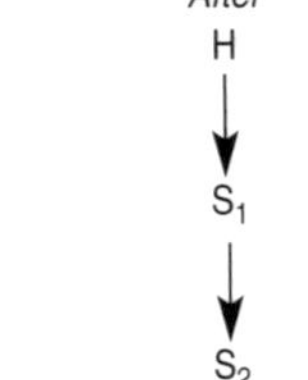

15: Continuing and discontinued interests

Topic List

IFRS 5 definitions

Non-current assets held for sale

Proforma disclosure

This topic is more likely to come up as part of a Section B question.

IFRS 5 *Non-current assets held for sale and discontinued operations* was published in 2004.

Definitions

Discontinued operation	A component of an entity that either has been disposed of or is classified as held for sale and: a) Represents a separate major line of business or geographical area of operations b) Is part of a single co-ordinated plan to dispose of a separate major line of business or geographical area of operations, or c) Is a subsidiary acquired exclusively with a view to resale
Component of an entity	Operations and cash flows that can be clearly distinguished, operationally and for financial reporting purposes, from the rest of the entity
Disposal group	A group of assets to be disposed of (by sale or otherwise) together as a group in a single transaction; **and** liabilities directly associated with those assets that will be transferred in the transaction
Asset held for sale	Its carrying amount will be recovered principally through sale rather than continuing use

Non-current assets held for sale

Criteria

- The asset (or disposal group) must be available for immediate sale in its present condition, subject only to usual and customary sales terms and
- The sale must be highly probable.

  For this to be the case:

  - The appropriate level of **management** must be **committed** to a plan to sell
  - An **active programme** to **locate a buyer** and complete the plan must have been initiated
  - The asset (or disposal group) must be **actively marketed** for sale at a price that is reasonable in relation to its current fair value
  - The sale should be expected to qualify for recognition as a completed sale **within one year** from the date of classification as held for sale (subject to limited specified exceptions)
  - Actions required to complete the plan should indicate that it is **unlikely** that **significant** changes to the plan will be made or that the plan will be withdrawn

Presentation

Assets and disposal groups (including associated liabilities) classified as held for sale are presented:

- In the SOFP
- Separately from other assets and liabilities
- Normally as **current** assets and liabilities (not offset)

Measurement

An entity must measure a non-current asset or disposal group classified as held for sale at the **lower of**:

- Carrying amount
- Fair value less costs to sell

Immediately before initial classifications, measure asset per applicable IFRS. Any impairment loss is accounted for as normal.

Non-current assets/disposal groups classified as held for sale are **not depreciated**.

Proforma disclosure

XYZ GROUP – STATEMENT OF PROFIT OR LOSS AND OTHER COMPREHENSIVE INCOME FOR THE YEAR ENDED 31 DECEMBER 20X3

	20X3	*20X2*
	$'000	$'000
Continuing operations		
Revenue	X	X
Cost of sales	(X)	(X)
Gross profit	X	X
Other income	X	X
Distribution costs	(X)	(X)
Administrative expenses	(X)	(x)
Other expenses	(X)	(X)
Finance costs	(X)	(X)
Share of profit of associates	X	X
Profit before tax	X	X
Income tax expense	(X)	(X)
Profit for the year from continuing operations	X	X
Discontinued operations		
Profit for the year from discontinued operations	X	X
Profit for the year	X	X
Profit attributable to		
Owners of the parent	X	X
Non-controlling interest	X	X
	X	X

16: Foreign currency transactions and entities

Topic List

- Introduction
- Individual entity stage
- Consolidated FS stage

Many large entities have subsidiaries overseas. In the exam you may well have to consolidate foreign subsidiaries.

There are two important concepts: functional currency and presentation currency. You need to know when and how to apply each.

IAS 21 also deals with the individual entity.

This topic was tested in 2008 and 2011 as a Section A question and in June 2014 as a Section B question.

Two currency concepts

Functional currency

- Currency of the primary economic environment in which an entity operates
- The currency used for measurement in the financial statements
- Other currencies treated as a foreign currency

Presentation currency

- Can be any currency
- Special rules apply to translation from functional currency to presentation currency
- Same rules used for translating foreign operations

During the period

- Translate each transaction at **exchange rate on date of transaction** (average rate (AR) for a period may be used as an approximation, if rates do not fluctuate significantly)
- Where the transaction is settled during the period the exchange difference arising is a realised gain or loss and is reported in profit or loss for the year

At the reporting date

- **Non-monetary assets** held at historic cost (non-current assets, inventory): remain at historical rate (HR)
- **Non-monetary assets** held at fair value (eg investments): exchange rate when fair value was determined
- **Monetary assets and liabilities:** restate at closing rate

Treatment of exchange differences

Part of profit/loss for the year

- On **trading transactions:** under 'other operating income or expense'
- On **financing transactions:** under 'finance income/finance cost'

Foreign operation shares functional currency of parent

An operation carries on its business as if it were an extension of the reporting entity, its results being more dependent on the economic environment of the investing entity's currency than its own reporting currency.

Consider:

- Whether the activities of the foreign operation are carried out as an **extension of the parent** or with a significant degree of autonomy
- Whether **transactions with the parent** are a **high or low proportion** of the foreign operation's activities
- Whether **cash flows** from the activities of the foreign operation directly affect the cash flows of the parent
- Whether the activities are financed from the foreign operation's own cash flows or by **borrowing from the parent**

Translate using same functional currency rules as for single entity, then consolidate

Foreign operation's functional currency is different from parent

The activities of the foreign operation are not an integral part of those of the reporting entity and its own economic environment and currency have most effect on its results.

Translate into parent's functional currency using presentation currency rules.

Steps	Method
1 Translate the **closing statement of financial position** (net assets/shareholders' funds) and use this for preparing the consolidated position statement in the normal way	Assets and liabilities – at **closing rate** Share capital and pre-acq'n reserves – at **historical rate** (at acq'n date) Post acq'n reserves – calculate as **balancing figure**
2 Translate the **statement of profit or loss and other comprehensive income (SPLOCI)** (Dividends should be translated at rate ruling when the dividend was paid.)	Use average rate. These figures can be used for the consolidated **SPLOCI**.

Steps

3 Take basic figures onto proforma answer

4 Calculate goodwill and any exchange difference arising

	C'000	C'000	Rate	$'000
Consideration transferred		X	HR	X
Non-controlling interests (at % FV of NA or 'full' fair value)		X	HR	X
Less: Fair value of net assets at acquisition				
Share capital	X			
Retained reserves	X			
		(X)	HR	(X)
Goodwill at acquisition		X	HR	X
Impairment losses 20X1		(X)	AR	(X)
Exchange gain/((loss) 20X1		–	J	X
Goodwill at 31 December 20X1		X	CR	X

Method

Goodwill is treated as an asset of the foreign subsidiary so although it is initially translated at the historical rate, it must be **restated to closing rate** at each year end and any exchange difference arising must be recognised at that point.

Steps	Method
5 Translate the **equity** (net assets) at the beginning of the year	Use the **closing rate** at the beginning of the year (the opening rate for the current year). This stage will be **unnecessary** if the question only requires a consolidated statement of financial position.
6 Calculate the **total exchange difference** for the year as follows	

	$
Closing net assets at closing rate (step 1)	X
Less opening net assets at opening rate (step 5)	X
	X

Steps

B/F	X
Less retained profit as translated (step 2)	X
Exchange differences	X/(X)
Group share (%)	X
Exchange difference on goodwill	X
(step 4)	X

Method

The exchange gain or loss arising in the year is recognised in **other comprehensive income**.

17: Group statements of cash flows

Topic List

IAS 7

Consolidated cash flows

If you get a statement of cash flows in an exam it will be a group cash flow statement, as you have covered individual companies in your earlier studies.

A group statement of cash flows is likely to appear as the first part of a compulsory 50 mark question, as happened in December 2010 and December 2013.

IAS 7 format

Inflows and outflows of cash of an entity are classified between the major economic activities.

- Operating activities
- Investing activities
- Financing activities

IAS 7 requires these notes.

- Property, plant and equipment: total acquisitions, analysed between finance leases and cash
- Cash and cash equivalents: cash, short-term investments and exchange rate movements
- Segment information: the total of each of the three cash flow headings by IFRS 8 segment

Definitions

Cash: cash on hand and demand deposits

Cash equivalents: short-term highly liquid investments that are readily convertible to known amounts of cash and which are subject to an insignificant risk of changes in value (generally < 3 month maturity).

What is a statement of cash flows for?

Information on cash flows assists the user in assessing entity's viability.

- Shows entity's cash generating ability
- Shows entity's cash utilisation needs

The statement required by IAS 7 is based on movement in cash and cash equivalents and can be criticised for not focusing on 'pure' cash.

Consolidated cash flows

Extra notes are required under investing activities

- Purchase or disposal of subsidiary
- Purchase or disposal of other business units

You won't need to do those in the exam

Non-controlling interest

Only the actual payment of cash, eg dividends, to non-controlling shareholders should be reflected in the cash flow statement. Include under 'cash flows from financing'.

Non-controlling interest	$'000
B/d – SOFP	X
SPLOCI (TCI attributable to NCI)	X
Dividends paid to NCI (balancing figure)	(**X**)
C/d – SOFP	X

Associates and joint-ventures (both equity accounted)

Only the actual cash flows from sales or purchases between the group and the entity, and investment in and dividends from the entity should be included.

- Dividends received should be included as a separate item in 'cash flows from investing activities'
- Separate disclosure of cash flows relating to acquisitions and investments
- Separate disclosure of financing cash flows between the reporting entity and equity-accounted investees

Investment in associates/JV	$'000
B/d – SOFP	X
SPLOCI – share of profit	X
SPLOCI – share of OCI	X
Acquisition/(disposal) of associate/JV	X/(X)
Exchange gain/(loss) on associate/JV	X/(X)
Dividends received from associate (balancing figure)	(**X**)
C/d	X

Acquisition or disposal of a subsidiary

Present as a simple item of cash inflow or outflow.

- Cash paid/received as consideration should be shown **net** of any cash transferred as part of the purchase/sale
- Must adjust other workings for:
  - Each asset/liability acquired or disposed of with the subsidiary
  - Non-cash elements of consideration, eg shares issued as part of the consideration
  - Cash/cash equivalents acquired/disposed
  - Other assets/liabilities acquired/disposed

You may get a statement of cash flows as part of the 50 mark case study question.

Notes

18: Environmental and social reporting

Topic List

- Environmental reporting
- Sustainability
- Integrated reporting
- Social responsibility
- Human resource accounting

These 'soft' issues deserve just as much attention as the more technical topics.

Environmental issues came up under the previous syllabus in connection with directors' social responsibility.

Environmental accounting

Environmental issues are likely to have a growing impact on business in the future due to forthcoming legislation, consumer pressure and so on.

What is environmental accounting?

- Recognising and seeking to mitigate the negative environmental effects of conventional accounting practice
- Separately identifying environmentally related costs and revenues within the conventional accounting systems
- Taking active steps to set up initiatives in order to ameliorate existing environmental effects of conventional accounting practice
- Devising new forms of financial and non-financial accounting systems, information systems and control systems to encourage more environmentally benign management decisions

What is environmental reporting?

- Developing new forms of performance measurement, reporting and appraisal for both internal and external purposes
- Identifying, examining and seeking to rectify areas on which conventional (financial criteria) and environmental criteria are in conflict
- Experimenting with ways in which sustainability may be assessed and incorporated into organisational orthodoxy

Impact on financial statements

No disclosure requirements relating to environmental issues at present. Some companies adopt voluntary disclosures (descriptive and unquantified) in the following areas.

- Contingent liabilities
- Exceptional charges
- Management Commentary comments
- Profit and capital expenditure forecasts

IAS 37 *Provisions, contingent liabilities and contingent assets* (see Chapter 9) addresses environmental liabilities (including site restoration costs).

Questions on environmental accounting are a good bet – you can always write something!

Pressure is mounting for companies to become more publicly accountable.

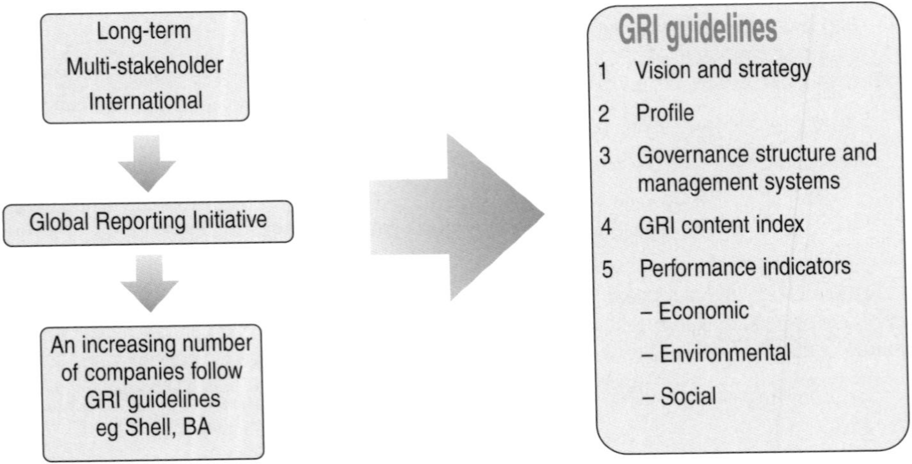

Long-term
Multi-stakeholder
International

Global Reporting Initiative

An increasing number of companies follow GRI guidelines eg Shell, BA

GRI guidelines

1 Vision and strategy
2 Profile
3 Governance structure and management systems
4 GRI content index
5 Performance indicators
   – Economic
   – Environmental
   – Social

Integrated Report

'A concise communication about how an organisation's strategy, governance, performance and prospects, in the context of its commercial, social and environmental context, leads to the creation and enchancement of value over the short, medium and long term.'

(IIRC)

Six categories of capital

Category	Characteristics
Financial	Funds available for use in the production of goods or the provision of services
Manufactured	Buildings, equipment or infrastructure used in the production of goods or the provision of services
Human	Skills, experience and motivation to innovate
Intellectual	Intangible assets providing competitive advantage (eg patents, copyrights, brand and reputation)
Natural	Inputs to goods and services, and natural environment on which organisation's activities have an impact (eg water, land, minerals, eco-systems)
Social	Institutions and relationships between stakeholders groups to enchance individual and collective well-being. Includes an organisation's social licence to operate

Environmental reporting | Sustainability | **Integrated reporting** | Social responsibility | Human resource accounting

IIRC: Seven guiding principles of IR

1. **Strategic focus and future orientation** – insight into strategy and how it relates to the use of the six capitals
2. **Connectivity** – holistic picture of relationships and dependencies
3. **Stakeholder relationships** – provide insight into the nature and quality of relationships, and how an organisation recognises and responds to stakeholders' interests
4. **Materiality** – only focus on matters which substantively affect organisation's ability to creat value
5. **Reliability and completeness** – present information in a balanced way, including negative matters as well as positive ones
6. **Conciseness** – report should be concise
7. **Consistency and comparability** – to enable comparison with other organisations

Key questions to address in an Integrated Report

- **Purpose** of organisation and **context** in which it operates
- **Governance** structure and how it supports organisation's ability to create value
- **Opportunities** and **risks** facing the organisation and how it is responding to them
- **Strategy** and **resource allocation**
- **Business model** – and how resilient it is to threats from the external environment
- **Performance** – how well has the organisation achieved its strategic objectives, and what effect has this had on the six capitals?
- **Future outlook** – what challenges and uncertainties is the organisation likely to face and what are the potential implications for these on its future performance?

Implications of IR

- Requirement for **forward-looking information** as well as historical
  - Insights into an organisation's prospects and future performance
  - But ... how much future information can/should an organisation provide?
- **Long-term performance** and business sustainability
  - Evaluate performance on a long-term basis as well as in the short-term
  - Performance measures need to promote a balance between long-term and short-term performance
  - Use of non-financial performance indicators
- **Value generation**
  - Focus on value generation (rather then narrow financial goals)
  - Increased use of non-financial data to gain a better understanding of performance
- **Insight into strategy**
  - Need to highlight the **significance** of figures, rather than simply **reporting** figures
- **Focus on key aspects of performance**
  - Guiding principle of **conciseness**: focus on aspects of performance which are truly key to the organisation's future success (critical success factors)

- **Stategic** – information needs to be more strategic; not just about historical, internal, financial performance
- **External information** – need information on external environment to highlight opportunities and threats
- **Requirement for non-financial information**
  - Can organisation's information systems supply the range of information stakeholders want to see?
  - Will systems need to be improved in order to enable the non-financial information to be collected?
  - Can the accountant ensure that non-financial information is reliable?
  - What **assurance** is there over non-financial information in a report?

Few organisations would admit to being irresponsible. However, **social responsibility** as practised by business is controversial. A socially responsible business engages in activities and incurs costs not very relevant to its business mission but which benefit society or groups within it.

Examples

- Charitable donations
- Secondment of staff to voluntary organisations
- Imposing stricter pollution limits than required by law
- Refusing to deal with suppliers who employ child labour

The stakeholder view of company objectives is that many groups of people have an interest in what the company does. Management must balance the profit objective with the pressures from the non-shareholder groups.

Environmental reporting | Sustainability | Integrated reporting | **Social responsibility** | Human resource accounting

Should social responsibility come at the expense of profit?

Against

- It's shareholders' money
- The business of business is making money; it's for governments to impose the law; raise taxes
- Society, not business, is the best judge of moral priorities and social welfare
- It's patronising to a workforce, whose lives might become controlled by the company

For

- Property rights are not the only rights
- Businesses get government support
- Externalities – businesses often don't pay the costs they impose on others
- Businesses are not just economic machines but social institutions
- Shareholders rarely exercise power
- Society is not just a market place
- Social responsibility is good PR
- Social responsibility pre-empts legislation

There are no right or wrong answers to this kind of question, but you must support your views with reasons.

Basic principle

- Employees are assets
- Competitive advantage is gained by effective use of people

Implications

- People are a resource
- Organisation must protect its investment
- Deterioration in attitudes is a cost to the company

Human asset accounting was developed, later broadened into **intellectual assets**.

Notes

19: Current developments

Topic List

- Current issues
- International harmonisation
- Move towards US GAAP

The examiner has a thing about current issues, so it is important that you are up to date with the latest developments.

Current issues | International harmonisation | Move towards US GAAP

Key topical issues

- Conceptual Framework Discussion Paper (Chapter 1)
- IFRS 9 Financial instruments (July 2014) (Chapter 7)
- 2013 ED on leasing (Chapter 8)
- IFRS 15 Revenue from contracts with customers (Chapter 1)
- ED Deferred tax for unrealised losses (Chapter 6)

To stay up to date keep an eye on *Student Accountant* magazine. Also ensure you visit the IASB and IAS Plus.com websites on a regular basis.

Barriers to harmonisation

- Language
- Different purposes of financial reporting
- Different legal systems
- Different user groups
- Needs of developing countries
- Nationalism
- Cultural differences
- Unique circumstances, eg hyperinflation
- Lack of strong accountancy bodies

Advantages of harmonisation

- Investors can compare results of different companies internationally
- Advantages for multinationals include:
  - Easier investment
  - Easier compliance
  - Easier to transfer accounting staff across national boundaries
- Governments of developing countries can adopt international standards for internal use
- Easier to promote cross border trade
- Large global accounting firms find multinational companies easier to audit

Dialogue with other key standard setters

- IASB has a policy of dialogue with key standard-setters around the world
- **China** has released accounting standards substantially converged with IFRS (2006)
- **Japan** announced a joint project with the IASB in 2005 to reduce differences
- Non-developed countries: not much progress

Convergence with US GAAP

- Convergence of FRS with IFRS is 'on hold' while IFRS converges with US GAAP
- 'Norwalk agreement' aims to reduce differences
- FASB recognised 'principles-based approach'
- Memorandum of Understanding signed with roadmap of convergence
- Convergence hindered by possibility of two different leasing standards

Progress on IFRS/US GAAP convergence

Major projects completed include:

Share-based payments	Substantially converged standards issued in 2004
Segment reporting	IFRS 8 *Operating segments* issued in 2006
Borrowing costs	Revised IAS 23 *Borrowing costs* issued in 2007
Business combinations	Joint requirements for business combinations and non-controlling interests issue in 2008 (IFRS 3 revised)
Conceptual framework	The project to develop a joint framework is still in progress but the chapters on objectives and qualititive characteristics were published in 2010

A March 2015 *Accountancy* article argued that the strong possibility of two different new leasing standards casts doubt on future convergence.

IFRS vs US GAAP

Some main differences are

Inventory

US allows LIFO, IFRS no longer does.

R & D

IFRS capitalises and amortises subject to strict criteria. US specifies write off.

Borrowing costs

US expensed.

IFRS says such costs must be capitalised.

The Securities and Exchange Commission did not indicate in its workplan that the US would adopt IFRS in the foreseeable future.

20: Reporting for specialised entities

Topic List

Your exam

Not-for-profit sector

IAS 41

Entity reconstructions

Questions will be set in terms of current IFRS.

Not-for-profit entities and smaller entities may have different accounting needs from the larger profit-making entities that you are used to.

Sometimes companies fail. A reconstruction scheme may be better than a liquidation.

Your exam

The examiner has stated explicitly that questions on specialised entities will be **set in terms of current IFRS**. So do not be alarmed if the setting is unusual – the principles will be the same.

Examples

- A sports club
- A college
- A health authority
- The edible oils industry

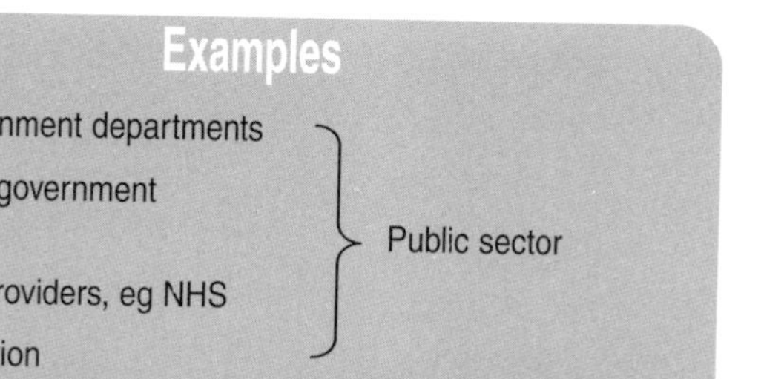

Not-for-profit entities have **different goals** from profit-making entities, but they still need to be **properly managed** and their accounts need to give a true and fair view.

Aims and conceptual framework

- IASB and FASB are working on a framework to include not-for-profit entities
  Problems
  - Different objectives
  - Different emphasis/definitions
- Accountability/stewardship important
- Primary user group is provider of funds
- Focus on cash flows
- Budgeting very important

Regulatory framework

- Local and national governments
- IASB and FASB framework

Performance measurement

- Emphasis on economy, efficiency and effectiveness, for **public sector** and key performance indicators
- **Charities** must demonstrate that they have made proper use of funds received

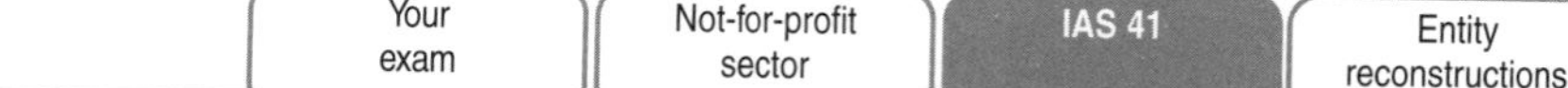

IAS 41 *Agriculture*

The aim of IAS 41 is to standardise the accounting treatment of biological assets (ie a living animal or plant) for valuation and recognition of gains and losses.

The IAS covers biologival assets from the point when the enterprise first acquires them until the point of harvest or slaughter.

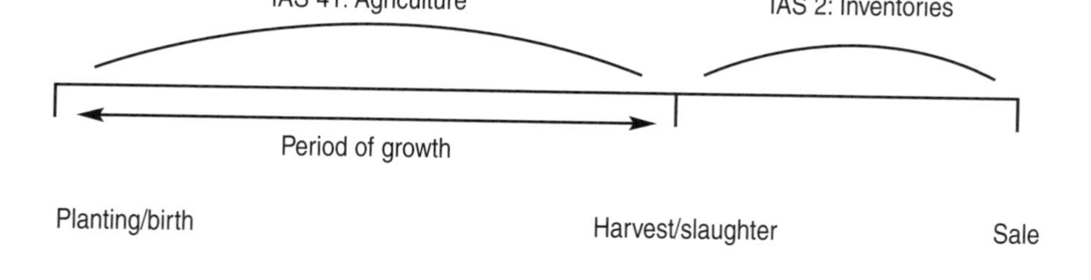

Recognition

Similar to other assets, biological assets are recognised when

- Controlled by the entity as a result of a past event
- Probable inflow of future economic benefits
- Cost or fair value can be measured reliably

Classification

- Biological assets are shown as **non-current** assets, in their own account category (broken down by immature and mature biological assets if material).

Measurement

- At each reporting date, biological assets are recognised at fair value less estimated point-of-sale costs
- Where there is no active market in homogenous biological assets, fair value is determined using most recent similar market price or sector benchmark valuation
- Otherwise, discounted cash flow is used to determine fair value
- If no reliable fair value method exists, historic cost less accumulated depreciation and impairment losses is used

Gains and losses

- Gain/loss on remeasurement to fair value is recognised in P/L

Most of your studies have been concerned with profitable businesses, but **occasionally businesses fail**.

Going concern – danger signs

- **Negative trends**: eg losses
- **Possible financial difficulties**: eg default on loan
- **Internal matters**: eg strikes
- **External matters**: eg lawsuits

Internal reconstructions

- **Must have a future** or liquidation would be preferable
- Any scheme **OK if legal** and creditors/shareholders agree
- **Must be fair** and have a chance of success

Steps

1. Open reorganisation account
2. Transfer shares/debentures to be replaced
3. Put through all asset write-downs/revaluations/expenses
4. Issue new shares from this account
5. Transfer balance to a capital reserve

Notes

21: Reporting for small and medium-sized entities

Topic List

- Big GAAP/Little GAAP
- IFRS for SMEs
- Areas of difference

Most companies are small, and have different accounting needs from the larger, listed companies for which IFRS was largely designed.

Big GAAP/Little GAAP

Most companies are **small** owned and managed by one person or family.

Should there be two GAAPs?

- Simple for smaller companies
- More detailed for longer ones

Possible solutions

- Differential reporting (standards specifically for smaller entities)
- Exemptions from IFRS or some requirements of IFRS

In the UK, the **FRSSE** was developed for small companies, ie companies below certain legally defined limits. In 2009, the IASB published the IFRS for SMEs. In 2013, the IFRS for SMEs was used as the basis for FRS 102, the Financial Reporting Standard applicable in the UK and Republic of Ireland, which replaced most of UK FRS.

IFRS for Small and Medium-sized Entities

- Published in 2009
- Applies to companies **without public accountability** (rather than using a size test)
- Much **less guidance** than full IFRS
- **Simplified recognition** and **measurement** rules
- **Only one option** where full IFRS gives a choice
- Topics **irrelevant** to SMEs **omitted**
- Significantly **fewer disclosures**
- Written in **clear language**
- ED in 2013 proposing **revisions**

Advantages: simpler, clearer, more relevant

Disadvantages: still onerous for very small companies, scope too wide, and there is room for further simplification

Key areas of difference – test yourself (look back to the text if you need to)

- Presentation and disclosure
- Financial instruments
- Investment property
- Property, plant and equipment
- Intangible assets
- Investments in subsidiaries and associates in the consolidated and separate accounts of the investor
- Government grants
- Borrowing costs
- Impairment of assets

Notes

Notes

Notes